THEOLOGIES OF POETRY

THEOLOGIES OF POETRY

POEMS, ESSAYS, AND IMAGES

ROBERT GIEBISCH

SHANTI ARTS PUBLISHING

BRUNSWICK, MAINE

THEOLOGIES OF POETRY

Published by Shanti Arts Publishing

Designed by Shanti Arts Designs

All photographs by Robert Giebisch
and used with his permission

All scripture excerpts are taken from the
KING JAMES VERSION, public domain.

Shanti Arts LLC
193 Hillside Road
Brunswick, Maine 04011

shantiarts.com

Printed in the United States of America

ISBN: 978-1-971191-10-2 (softcover)
ISBN: 978-1-971191-11-9 (hardcover)

LCCN: 2026937309

To Allison and Danny,
may you find your way.

Contents

Acknowledgements / 11
Preface / 13

SEEKING

poems: Before Names Are Spoken / 16
Peaches / 17
Dählhölzli, Bern, Switzerland, June 2023 / 18
Conversation with the Ferns / 20
Toward Breath / 21
Doubt / 22
Forest Spring / 23
Salceda Prairie Grass / 24
Simple Soup / 25
Hudson Psalm / 26
Without You / 27
My Secret, Crans-Montana Summer Camp,
   Switzerland, July 1971 / 28
Solitude / 30
Mindfulness / 31
Zazen / 32
Way of the Leaf / 34
Aare River, Bern, Switzerland / 35
Volubilis, Morocco, March 2016 / 36
Still, We Hold / 37
Your Eminence / 38
Hypnos / 39
Five More Minutes of Illusion / 40
Helianthus / 42
Dancing / 43
Boyhood Bedroom / 44
Tai Chi in the Backyard / 46

essay: Sacred Ground / 49

LISTENING

poems: Kenai Fireweed, August 2025 / 64

Weightless Form / 66

Nature's Breath / 67

Scent of the Camino / 68

Sol Invictus / 70

Forest Sleep / 72

Psalm 23 / 73

Backyard Sutra / 75

Praying on a Winter Day / 76

Lord Have Mercy / 77

Hallelujah / 78

Russian River, August 2024 / 79

San Pedro, Belize, December 2024 / 81

Saint-Saëns's *The Swan* for Cello, July 2004 / 82

Church of Fog / 83

Gjirokastër, Albania, November 2024 / 84

Syri i Kalter, Albania, November 2024 / 86

essay: My Mother and the Tao / 89

REJOICING

poems: Sunday, Near Bethesda Fountain, Central Park / 96

Yuletide / 98

Twelfth Night / 99

Forest Games / 100

Soup Kitchen Prayer / 101

Offerings to the Exercise Gods / 102

Union Square Market, Saturday / 103

Smiling on a Winter Day / 104

Fugue at Daybreak / 105

Orangutan Meets Heidegger,
    Tanjung Puting, Borneo, Indonesia, 2025 / 106

Bornean Clouded Leopard, Night Along
    the Sekonyer, October 2025 / 107

Incarnation / 108

Chestnut and Bamboo, Woodbridge,
    Connecticut, Winter 2024 / 110
Roadside Banquet / 112
Water Falling / 113
Words and Pictures / 114
Let Not Your Hearts Be Troubled / 116

ACCEPTING

essay: My Father / 121

poems: Christ in Linden / 136
    Flushing, Queens / 137
    San Francisco / 138
    Gazing out My Window / 140
    Climate Blues / 141
    Inshallah / 142
    Sages / 144
    Methuselah / 146
    By My Mother's Grave / 147
    Far Away / 148
    On Attending Jon's Memorial or Petals Falling / 149
    Komodo Dragon Tour, Indonesia / 150
    Old Man Monk, Burma, January 2006 / 151
    Queens Bound, 14th Street, January 6, 2024 / 152
    On Visiting Borobudur, Java, October 2025 / 154
    Walking with an Old Friend, Sperry Falls,
        Woodbridge, Connecticut / 157
    Egyptian Revival, West 70th Street / 158
    Time and Earth / 161
    On Visiting the Statue of Liberty, March 29, 2025 / 163

essay: The Camino de Santiago:
        Journals of Spiritual Convergence / 165

About the Author / 203

Acknowledgements

My deepest thanks go to my dear friends Jefferson Singer and Robert Livingston, who read my roughest drafts and offered their most honest feedback; to my wife, Ninrong, whose steady encouragement, common sense, and quiet wisdom guided me through every page; to my children, Allison and Danny, who inspired me to pass this journey on to the next generation; and to my sister Christina, my spiritual co-traveler over many seasons of life.

I am especially grateful to my parents, without whom this book would not exist. My mother, Ilse, first opened my eyes to Buddhism and Taoism. My father, Gerhard, encouraged me to read history and philosophy with curiosity and an open mind.

The members of the New Haven Chapter of the Connecticut Poetry Society and my hometown writers group of Woodbridge, Connecticut, deserve special praise for their thoughtful insights and generous criticism. I am particularly indebted to Christine Beck, Tony Fusco, Bill Moorhead, Karl Traichel, Amy Graver, Peter Ulisse, Kevin Carey, Mary Lachman, Marguerite Dillaway, Lorri Danzig, Mariah Evans, Meredith Kazer, Janet Blair, David Hudnall, Timothy Chegwidden, and Caty Poole.

I also wish to offer special thanks to Christine Cote of Shanti Arts for her skillful and professional work in designing this book, and for her graceful integration of my poetry, prose, and photography.

Preface

I've often wondered why I write so many poems about God. I don't consider myself a particularly religious person.

As a boy in our Congregational church in New England, I spent most Sundays trying not to giggle as a choir of middle-aged women sang hymns in warbling vibratos, while otherwise rational men listened dutifully to an aging minister drone on about someone—or something—we could neither see nor touch. It all seemed suspect. Religion appeared to be either a convenient way to prod people into moral behavior or a ruse to soothe our loneliness and soften the certainty of death in an indifferent universe.

And yet, here I am, writing poems about "God."

What does that word even mean? Can anyone truly define it? I've never found an answer that satisfied me. Hence, poetry, or what I've come to call theologies of poetry.

Why "theologies"? From the Greek *Theos* (God) and *logos* (word): thinking and speaking about the divine. Though the term is often tied to Christianity, I use it in a broader sense, as the expression of our felt relationship to whatever we might call spirit. By pairing theology with poetry, I hope to widen its compass, to make space for those deeply non-rational ways we sense the sacred.

Ah yes, definitions. Is God an impersonal clockmaker? An intimate listener who answers our prayers? Nature, Love, the Tao, the Way, emptiness itself, a projection, a shared illusion, an opiate? I don't know. But I do know I keep returning.

I've spent a lifetime traveling far and wide, only to find myself back at my doorstep—the quiet room of the poet—where I try to speak into the silence what it means to search for God. Monotheism, polytheism, folk tradition, pantheism, Buddhism, Taoism, Christianity—all find their place here.

I hope these poems as well as a handful of essays on sacred ground, pilgrimage, and family will resonate with readers who, like many, claim little allegiance to organized religion yet still long for a spiritual dimension in life. The final piece, on the Camino de Santiago, weaves prose and poetry into a single meditation on the journey of the soul.

Woodbridge, Connecticut
March 2026

ONE

SEEKING

Before Names Are Spoken

serving you coffee
in bed this morning
tiptoeing in the dark

the mug warm
your breath still slow
beneath flannel sheets

I stay a moment
watch the steam rise
between us

your hand stirs
as though remembering
and I—almost bow

outside,
frost halos
the window's edge

Peaches

Back door unlatched,
breakfast plates
still on the counter.

Front door—
a bag of peaches,
skin flushed gold,

each meant
for her friend
whose brain swells,

cell on cell,
spirals tightening
at the core.

I stand there,
as if my standing
might keep our house safe.

Dählhölzli, Bern, Switzerland, June 2023

wisteria frame
the forest path—
passage to another world

the trunks lean inward
not touching—
a space between them
holds the light

ferns tremble
where the air narrows—
as if something
has just passed through

my steps grow quieter
the farther I go—
each branch ahead
more finely drawn

and still, it opens—
this corridor of green
pulling me forward
on the breath of leaves

Conversation with the Ferns

they never interrupt
just unfold
frond by frond
as if revealing nothing
was the point all along

their green
not loud,
but certain

they lean toward the window
without expecting it to open

I speak aloud sometimes
just to see
if silence has a shape

one rustles—
not in answer
but in patience

Toward Breath

a reed leans west in the wind
knowing how the river turns

no prayer is spoken
just a hush between leaf and water

a dragonfly pauses
midair, barely moving

light skims the surface
slips away

a fish darts under a stone
quick as forgetting

I hope—not with hands clasped,
but with center opening

to hold what won't stay—
Ruach, Qi—

the drift between heartbeats
where quiet gathers

where a gaze meets mine,
and breathes through me.

Doubt

flags to the heavens
drop one by one—
the oak stands naked

wind moves freely
through what was hidden,
rattling twigs—

fingers caught in prayer
each branch a question
still reaching

Forest Spring

My soul drifts—
a murmur of dream and feeling,
drinking green silence
to fullness.

Moss gathers
where words would fall,
soft as prayer
never spoken.

Light filters down
in braided strands—
a slow annunciation
through the trees.

Roots press deeper
than memory,
each step
a kind of remembering.

Here,
nothing asks
and nothing hurries.
Even the wind
knows how to kneel.

And I—
less visitor
than echo—
remain
until breath and branch
move as one.

Salceda Prairie Grass

you never speak

just lean when wind
touches your necks

a stillness passes through you
like thought in sleep

held by your roots
you yield, then rise

light slips away,
you turn silver

returning
to your original shape

Simple Soup

I pour
metal scrapes metal
steam rises
bowl after bowl
knuckles weathered
handles worn

a thin man waits
our eyes meet
my wrist dips twice
the line moves on
my hands remembering
what words forget

Hudson Psalm

your winds from the West
ripple across the Hudson

anointing my face
folding my name into water

carrying it without weight—
each syllable unbraiding

Without You

watering your amaranths
their roots moist—
your steps far away

threads of water
vanish
at each stem's base

no sound—
just the ache
of something taken

My Secret, Crans-Montana Summer Camp, Switzerland, July 1971

I found a rowboat tipped on its side
beneath the alders near the pier.

Why not?

I slid it into the water,
stepped in, took the oars.

My arms, long and almost strong
in that teenage kind of way,
pulled me across the lake—

yes, it was stealing.
Or maybe borrowing.
Either way, I kept rowing.

A strange calm, stillness, and then—
a spill of light,
not golden, but bone-white,
the kind that makes you squint
and stop thinking.

I floated in it,
not asking forgiveness,
not needing permission—

just drifted,
emptied,
witnessed.

I brought the boat back,
tied it to the post,

walked up the hill,
as if nothing had happened.

Solitude

a grayish morning—
I dance alone on the pier

I lift my arms
into the chill—
no branch, no wing
only fog
and the water's murmur

something shifts
beyond the wind—
cool on my cheek
against my skin

light slips
through the clouds
warms my face—
the river keeps breathing

Mindfulness

thoughts wander
chipmunks—
another one darts by

a leaf curls
on the edge of the path
its shadow still

tree roots
cross the trail
slick with last night's rain

a fly brushes
my skin
then lifts

gravel shifts
beneath each step

Zazen

the *keisu* fades
a low hum lingers

a siren wails—
I find my still point

the pitch climbs
levels
thins

drawn out
beyond hearing

air holds it—
a ringing
without source

Way of the Leaf

A leaf turns twice
before it lands,
spiraled down
by unseen hands.

Your breath beside me
in morning's chill,
the world spins gently—
we walk uphill.

Aare River, Bern, Switzerland

"S" wriggles
across the river's skin—
currents draw calligraphy

yin-yang drifts past
spinning slowly
in a boy's cupped hands

bare feet on stone—
he watches it turn,
then lets it go

Volubilis, Morocco,
March 2016

skipping—
tunnels yelling
echoes chasing me

a child's laugh—
or mine,
before I was born

stones remember
what I forget—
the trace of sandals
brushed into dust

what runs before me
isn't fear
but something older
than speech—

a name
just out of reach

Still, We Hold

begonias—heads drooping
dreaming of water cans
we, too, feel neglected

we were blooming yesterday
soft and angled just so

one of us tilted too far
but caught herself in time

the sun moved
and no one noticed

a glass was filled
but not for us

still, we hold our silence
better than some—

wilting, yes,
but with restraint

Your Eminence

the cardinal visits—
a flash of red
at the corner of my eye

he perches
on the garden gate
as if expected

I nod
he tilts his head—
neither of us blinks

then off he goes
leaving no blessing
just one feather

Hypnos

I draw the quilt to my chin
knees curled as they were
at nine or ten—
when my days felt held

back when I'd kneel
in the grass with my soldiers
lining them up in the dirt
beneath the maple

a marble in my pocket
cool and smooth—
shadows shifting
across the lawn

now I lie still
and walk that yard again—
the war already won
my breath in rows
falling into rhythm

Five More Minutes of Illusion

beneath a comforter
in my cave

avoiding Plato's light
leaves flicker on the wall

I turn away
truth waiting on the other side

Helianthus

sunflowers—
their faces
eavesdropping on us

we spoke low
beneath their crowns
as if secrets could hold

stems creaked
in the heat
but none turned away

you laughed
and picked one
without looking

I watched
its shadow fall
across us

Dancing

West Side din—
wild grasses sway
as if the taxis
were singing to them

horns flare,
gears stammer—
they bow,
adjust,
graceful in the pause

no wind,
only the long murmur
of trucks

still, they move—
untroubled
by the source

Boyhood Bedroom

French West Africa,
the Portuguese in Angola, the British in Belize—
the US in Panama, too.

A 1950s globe
in a white boy's room,
a stone's throw in time

from Cook and Lewis and Clark
to Fremont and Stanley,
and Leopold's ivory and rubber, too.

Pax Americana—
he climbed the Colossus
in sneakers and wonder,

dizzy
with *terra incognita*,
Indochine in italics,
the Other—
heat and hush and lust,
a monk's quiet.

A boy's dream
of empire and distance,
spread in storybook colors.

Maps and atlases,
bound Britannicas,
the luster of old names

recalled in shame—
evaporated in guilt,
desiccated,
pressed
between pages—
in the back of his room.

Tai Chi in the Backyard

invisible ball
gathered at my core

a slow punch
through autumn air

scatters one yellow leaf
sends another turning

my heel sinks
into the ground—
weight not held, but placed

arms unfold
as if drawn
from the center

the spine steadies—
the hands recall

Sacred Ground

This book is a record of convergences—of places, images, silences, and inward movements that have shaped the poems I've written. This essay arises from the intuition that place is not merely setting, but sacrament, a threshold where landscape, memory, and spirit conspire to generate meaning.

The five locations described here—some urban, some wild, some sacred by human design, others by suffering or sheer presence—have not only influenced me personally; they have entered my poems. I privilege these places because, at least for me, they emit a spiritual valence. Hence, my need to return to them in what might be called "pilgrimages." I have visited all of them more than once, some many times.

"The Lord is my shepherd," Psalm 23 reads, "I shall not want. He maketh me to lie down in green pastures. He leadeth me beside the still waters. He restoreth my soul." These lines capture the essence of what I hope to convey: that certain "pastures" and "waters" offer us peace, perhaps even something just short of enlightenment. A mystical force—call it God, or Tao, or Buddha, or Dharma—seems to draw us to such places. Many of us carry these longings deep within.

The first sacred place I would like to share is **FORT TRYON PARK AND THE CLOISTERS**, perched on the banks of the Hudson River in Manhattan. This medieval collection of French, Italian, Spanish, and Austrian relics came into being in the 1930s. When I first laid eyes on it in the 1960s, I was just a boy. Reaching the Cloisters from our home meant passing through Fort Tryon Park, named for the last British general to govern New York at the

outbreak of the American Revolutionary War. Margaret Corbin Drive, the turnabout at the park's entrance, bears the name of the American woman patriot wounded while fighting British troops here in 1776.

As a child, Sunday strolls to Fort Tryon Park were the high point of our week. My sister and I scampered over boulders, shouted into tunnels to hear our voices echo, and often ended up in the heather garden marveling at its azaleas, daylilies, lavenders, and tulips. We climbed up to Linden Terrace, overlooking the

Hudson River, where the view westward across the Hudson still awes me to this day.

Less frequently, our family would continue north to the Cloisters. There, striking courtyards, gurgling fountains, beds of medicinal herbs, and medieval relics greeted us. My favorite was always the tomb effigy of the knight of the d'Aluye family from the Loire Valley, hidden deep within the museum. He died in the mid-thirteenth century after returning from a crusade to the Holy Land. His hands are folded in prayer, his shield and sword immortalized in limestone, a lion lying at his feet. Knight and lion lie together in what seems an eternal repose, a quiet embodiment of dignity, humility, and a courage that asks for nothing in return.

After we moved from Manhattan, I continued to visit Fort Tryon Park and the Cloisters. Soon after I met Ninrong, my wife, I brought her here. When we were raising Allison and Danny, I made sure they had the chance to wander through the Cloisters as well.

Once, after a hurricane, I crossed the park by foot, stepping over fallen branches and ducking under toppled trees, and, yes, ignoring NYPD sawhorses along the way. When we emerged on the far side, an officer greeted us, and I had some explaining to do. Claiming I needed to traverse sacred ground didn't quite cut it.

These days, when I spend weekends in the city and need a quick escape from downtown's hustle and bustle, I hop a subway to Washington Heights and wander through the heather gardens of Fort Tryon Park. Beneath those gardens lies an elegant, arched tunnel, a remnant of the Gilded Age, when the Billings Estate (long since lost to fire) stood high above the Hudson. Passing through that tunnel feels like entering a cathedral in Europe.

In August 2024, Allison's fiancé proposed to her here. This tunnel even appears in my dreams, having made recurring guest appearances across the decades. For me, the earth beneath that tunnel has always been sacred ground.

Second stop on this tour of sacred places: the **Dählhölzliwald**, a riverside forest along the Aare in Bern, Switzerland.

In 1966 our family moved to Bern, and I entered third grade at the public school in Elfenau, a district overlooking the snow-capped Bernese Oberland. Just a few blocks from our apartment I discovered what felt like an enchanted wood. On clear days the distant peaks of the Eiger, Mönch, and Jungfrau stood sentinel; in the foreground lay the Dählhölzliwald, a carefully tended park on our side of the Aare. Paths were swept clean of twigs and overgrowth, beds of pine needles cushioned ancient evergreens, and the river's turquoise water rushed down from the Alps. Farther downstream, a small zoo housed Alpine ibex, mountain goats with sweeping, scimitar-shaped horns.

Whenever I stepped beneath the trees, a gentle safety enfolded me. Multiplication tables and German poetry evaporated. I surrendered to the timeless beauty of Nature with a capital "N."

Years later I returned again. In high school, while studying in Geneva, I managed several pilgrimages. After my medical internship at Stanford, I stopped at the Dählhölzliwald on the way back from an Alpine trek with my father. In 2007 I brought Ninrong, Allison, and Danny, then slipped out alone at dawn to watch the Aare crest, just shy of flood stage. In May 2023 Danny and I walked the forest twice during a brief Swiss visit. The Dählhölzliwald now boasts new paths and welcoming benches where one can stretch, gaze across the open fields, and willingly lose track of time.

A classic sacred place, indeed.

Our third stop: **Preah Vihear Temple**, perched high atop a remote escarpment on the Thai-Cambodian border.

Yes, we leap from the tidy forests of Switzerland to the tangled jungles of Southeast Asia.

I first discovered Preah Vihear in the summer of 2009 during a trip to Cambodia with Ninrong and Danny. In Phnom Penh, patriotic billboards depicting the temple caught my eye. I had never imagined such a place existed. My curiosity was piqued.

Back in the United States, I began researching. I learned that Preah Vihear is an ancient Hindu temple built by the Khmer Empire between the ninth and eleventh centuries of the Common Era and dedicated to Shiva in his manifestation as Sikharesvara, the mountain deity. The temple symbolizes Mount Meru, the mythic center of the cosmos in Hindu belief. And indeed, it stands atop a 1,722-foot cliff in the Dângrêk Mountains, offering what may be the most spectacular setting of any Khmer temple.

Preah Vihear has long been contested by Thailand and Cambodia, its stones scarred by history. As recently as 2011, the Thai army shelled the temple grounds. In the 1970s, after the fall of the Khmer Rouge, retreating fighters occupied Preah Vihear, and to this day, landmines remain scattered in the surrounding terrain.

But perhaps the most harrowing episode came in 1979, when the Thai military forcibly expelled approximately 42,000 Cambodian refugees by driving them toward the cliffs of Preah Vihear. Unloaded from buses, the refugees were forced down the steep escarpment without paths, without guidance. Some hid atop the cliff and survived. Others were shot or thrown off the edge. Most climbed, using vines as ropes, children tied to their backs or strapped across their chests. As they descended, Thai soldiers rolled boulders after them.

At the base of the cliff, Khmer Rouge minefields awaited. The safest path was marked not by signs but by the bodies of those who had gone before, refugees who had triggered the landmines and, in dying, unwittingly marked a narrow corridor to safety.

I visited Preah Vihear twice, on New Year's Day 2010 and again in February 2013, each time traveling alone with a Cambodian driver. Thai troops had shelled the site shortly before my first visit, and unexploded ordnance still ringed the temple in 2013.

So, you ask: what inspired me, a middle-aged family man, to visit this remote, battle-scarred corner of the Earth?

In 2010, Preah Vihear remained far off the tourist map. I was captivated by the thought of standing on the edge of a cliff with an ancient Hindu-Buddhist temple at my back, gazing out across the Cambodian plains. I believed something inside me might change if I made it there. And yes, the dark legacy of the Khmer Rouge drew me in; this was sacred ground, a symbol of Mount Meru, the mythic home of the gods, and witness to unimaginable human suffering below.

As Psalm 23 reads: "Yea, though I walk through the valley of the shadow of death, I will fear no evil: for thou art with me; thy rod and thy staff they comfort me." Perhaps, for me, venturing to Preah Vihear was a way of walking through that valley.

At the time, I was writing a novel, *Cambodian Time*, about gangsters, soldier-monks, and a half-crazed psychiatrist who vanishes at Preah Vihear, only to reemerge, after many misadventures, transformed. Several scenes took place at the temple. The manuscript remains unpublished.

On that first journey, I traveled hundreds of miles north of Phnom Penh on partially paved roads through dense jungle, terrain that, by my second visit, had been cleared for coconut oil plantations. I spent the night in a bare-bones hotel in Tbaeng Meanchey and wandered the dimly lit night market, the only foreigner in sight. Everything was cash only. I kept close watch over my documents.

The next morning we ascended the switchback road up the Dângrêk escarpment. Halfway up, our truck overheated and stalled. Only after pouring several liters of water into its belly did we coax it back to life. At the temple gate, we were greeted by several troops of surprisingly cheerful Cambodian soldiers armed with automatic rifles. I never quite knew what they made of me.

The temple itself is composed of five sanctuaries, or *gopuras*, arranged along a gradual incline. Each one blocks the view of the next, so that no single vantage point reveals the whole. As I wandered through the complex, a group of young soldiers sang softly nearby. One played a traditional Khmer xylophone, shaped like a curved wooden boat. Step by step, I passed through the *gopuras* until I emerged into a clearing at the southern edge.

There the land fell away into a sheer drop, no railing, no fence, and below, the vast plains of Cambodia stretched into a hazy distance. The air shimmered with heat and smoke from countless controlled burns. With the temple behind me, facing the open expanse of jungle and fields, I stood still.

I knew I had reached sacred ground.

Three years later, in February 2013, I returned to Preah Vihear. The second visit stirred me just as deeply as the first. I hope to stand there again before my life is done.

Our next stop: **GOLDEN GATE PARK IN SAN FRANCISCO, CALIFORNIA**, which I first encountered in 1982 at the start of medical school at the University of California, San Francisco (UCSF).

The moment I stepped into the park and inhaled the citrusy scent of eucalyptus, I knew I had entered a special place. Miles of gently winding paths rolled westward toward the Pacific, weaving through a dazzling array of landscapes and landmarks: the Japanese Tea Garden, the San Francisco Botanical Garden, the Conservatory of Flowers, Stow Lake, Strawberry Hill, and Huntington Falls.

During the early 1980s, when I attended UCSF, Golden Gate Park became one of my closest companions. Long jogs and meandering hikes through the park helped me manage the stress of medical school. While memorizing anatomy, pathology, microbiology, and pharmacology, I knew that I could always walk a few steps down from Mount Parnassus where UCSF stood, take a jog in the park, visit the Japanese Tea Garden to sip a meditative cup of green tea, or even run all the way to the ocean and watch the waves roll in and crash against the shore. The park's nearness to the sea made it especially compelling. I always savored standing on the beach and gazing westward, imagining myself flying to Thailand, from where I had only just recently returned.

That Haight-Ashbury, just east of Golden Gate Park, had once served as one of the epicenters of the 1960s counterculture movement made the park even more alluring. Lying on the grass on a sunny day, I would close my eyes and imagine drifting off to a different time and place. The irony is that, as a second-year medical student, I sat for my first National Board of Medical Examiners test at the San Francisco Botanical Garden in the park. This exam is a grueling, daylong rite of passage before students move on to their clinical rotations in their third and fourth years. I recall taking a lunch break that day and gazing off into the Botanical Garden, calmed and steadied by the quiet presence of its radiant foliage.

After I graduated from UCSF and returned east to settle in Connecticut, I began to dream of Golden Gate Park. In my dreams, the park and the neighborhoods surrounding it took on a magical quality. I imagined moving back, envisioning San Francisco as a promised land that extended north and south along the California coast. Sunny skies, breathtaking cliffs, banks of clouds suspended above the Pacific—if only I had chosen San Francisco over Connecticut, I told myself, I would be happy. Subsequent visits to the city and the passage of time have tempered those idealized visions of the city, but I still cherish the park. For me, it remains sacred ground.

In the autumn of 2019, a few months before the pandemic struck, Ninrong and I visited San Francisco for one of her pathology conferences. While she took her sessions, I drove across town to pay homage to Golden Gate Park. My visit included a pilgrimage to the San Francisco Botanical Garden, or Arboretum, where the city's mild Mediterranean climate allows a profusion of nearly 9,000 species to grow. Palms, conifers, magnolias, and even cloud forest species thrive along its carefully tended paths and quiet ponds.

I happened to visit the park on a crystal-clear, blue-sky weekday morning. I had almost the entire Arboretum to myself. I passed through the Andean Cloud Forest and the Rhododendron Garden, eventually arriving at the banks of the Waterfowl Pond, where several ducks floated quietly past. I stood still and gazed up the lawn toward the Ancient Plant Forest, with its palm-like cycads and conifers. I could almost imagine dinosaurs roaming the park.

At that moment, I realized that I had reached sacred ground. What more could one ask for? Fancy food? Exotic trips? Baubles? First editions? Here was everything worth seeking. Plants, water, sky, and

animals in perfect harmony. My pulse relaxed. My blood pressure dropped. I took several long, deep breaths. No need to close my eyes.

Thank you, thank you, God, I thought.
How lucky I am, just to stand here and breathe this air.

From the Arboretum, I hiked past Stow Lake and wandered toward the Pacific, only to retrace my steps and end at the Japanese Tea Garden beneath the Buddha statue cast in 1790 in Tajima

Province, known as Amazarashi-no-Hotoke, or "the Buddha that sits throughout the sunny and rainy weather without shelter."

I love to stand beneath that larger-than-life bronze figure and gaze up into its serene face. It fills me with a deep sense of peace and quiet joy, no matter what mood I might be in. Moods, like the weather, shift and pass. That Buddha remains still, "ready but relaxed," as my tai chi teacher would say.

Another sacred space.

Final stop: **CENTRAL PARK AND THE METROPOLITAN MUSEUM OF ART**. Over the past several years, I've come to know them as well as my backyard. I've visited so often that, rather than call them "pilgrimages," it might be more accurate to think of them as "walking meditations."

One of my favorite pastimes is to wander across Central Park on an early weekday morning after a rainstorm, when the air is still fresh, and the morning dew has not yet lifted from the trees and grass. The weekend crowds are absent, and the park's paths, statues, and ponds lie in a kind of pristine silence. When I pass someone in the park, they are more likely to smile. An early morning innocence seems to rest gently over everything.

What I cherish most about Central Park is the way that Frederick Law Olmsted designed it. Surrounded by a city layout of rectangles, he made sure Central Park would be laced with winding bridle paths and curved roads. Whether I'm hiking in the Ramble, rowing a boat on The Lake, or sitting on a bench in the gazebo on Rocky Hill, I feel poised at the threshold where nature meets city. Through its statues, reservoirs, and roads, the park immerses us in nature, but in a way that is aesthetically shaped, even orchestrated. And as I reflect on this survey of sacred places, I'm struck by how all of them are, in some sense, parks, whether Fort Tryon Park, the Dählhölzliwald, Golden Gate Park, Central Park, or even Preah Vihear. Though not technically a park, it too blends architecture with a dramatic natural setting.

I hesitate to identify specific spots in Central Park as sacred ground because, in a certain sense, the entire park serves that meaning for me. Although I might love the stillness of an early weekday morning, I also delight in sauntering across the park on a busy summer afternoon when tourists from around the world flood it with their accents and unfamiliar tongues. I love entering these human streams, flowing with them through the park's verdant splendor, catching snippets of conversation and admiring the shifting clusters of people drifting past. I feel part of something larger than myself.

That said, I cannot resist naming one spot in Central Park that I find especially enchanting: the Shakespeare Garden. Whenever I visit, I'm reminded of these lines from *A Midsummer Night's Dream:*

> *I know a bank where the wild thyme blows,*
> *Where oxlips and the nodding violet grows;*
> *Quite over-canopied with luscious woodbine,*
> *With sweet musk-roses and with eglantine,*
> *There sleeps Titania sometime of the night,*
> *Lull'd in these flowers with dances and delight.*

Yes, a sense of romance pervades the Shakespeare Garden. I love to watch its rich beds blossom in spring and blaze in full summer glory, only to wither and fade with the autumn rains. I even visit it in the depths of winter to read the Shakespeare quotes beneath the bare stems whose petals once bloomed.

I think of Ninrong and how much I love her, and how she enjoys gardening. When we visit together, we get to savor the flowers without the planting, watering, and weeding that's required back home. I'm filled with a deep sense of gratitude—that nature provides these flowers, that the Park offers this refuge, and that we are well enough to walk and wonder.

Yes, sacred ground indeed.

For me, the Metropolitan Museum of Art is a temple of sorts. It would take a lifetime to absorb all its wonders. Over the years, I've found one room especially meaningful. The Astor Court, also called the Ming Hall, is a re-creation of a Ming dynasty-style garden courtyard. When I stand there, I feel transported to a time and place where mind and body blend with rock and water, an imaginary landscape of mountains and lakes. I close my eyes and feel as though I'm wandering through a quiet valley in China.

Another sacred space.

There are many other locations that I might honor as sacred. And perhaps that's the deeper point: that any place may become sacred, even, or perhaps especially, those we visit daily. Why wait for five sites in the world? Life is too short for such restraint. But I do find these five especially powerful, as they embody a vital meeting point between nature and art, between what the earth offers freely and what we have done to honor its gifts.

So, I will continue to cherish every chance I get to make pilgrimages to these places.

And I will always savor the opportunity to walk on sacred ground.

TWO

LISTENING

Kenai Fireweed, August 2025

Eighteen thousand years ago
we knelt, gathered petals,

magenta flares on blackened ash,
fires after conflagrations,

listening, earth remembering.

Now my granddaughter breathes,
fists uncurling, first cries.

Fireweed flares
against the char,

my hands reach for its leaves.
She coos and babbles,

where seeds once fell.

Weightless Form

holding the intangible ball
summer slips by

shifting weight
heel to toe

shadows lengthen
on the garden wall

the breath settles
without command

elbows float,
knees recall

a thread from crown
to earth

silence coils
between each turn

palms open—
nothing held

Nature's Breath

lichen darkens
on the stone wall—
as if the stone
had drawn a breath.

leaves drip
without wind
each drop
a soft decision.

moisture beads
along the bark's spine—
hesitates,
then slips away.

beneath the moss
water slides sideways,
changing course
like thought.

Scent of the Camino

the path warms early—
eucalyptus in the air

a second scent rises—
low, wet, sweet

hoof prints in mud
a sparrow drops into a rut,
vanishes

leaf, dung,
resin, steam—
a gate swings

a dog sleeps
in a tractor's shadow,
a fruit stand leans into the ditch—
no one there

peaches in a crate,
bees circling the bruised ones

there must be more—
something better—

but then:

a woman kneels at a stream,
wets her scarf,
twists it once,
lays it on her neck

two goldfinches quarrel,
go still—
as if they forgot

a chapel stands open
inside:

a candle flickers,
a chair off-center,
wax nearly gone

outside—
a question mark
chalked on stone,
half-faded

Sol Invictus

Daybreak on the ridge
warms these fingers,
keeps this autumn heart alive.

I raise my head, eyes closed,
and a stillness—
not wind, not breath—
just light,
steady as a pulse,
settles through me.

Forest Sleep

our breath joins
the rhythm of needles falling—
soft as lichen
closing over stone

trunks lean inward,
gathered like elders
around warmth
rising from the ground

leaf-shadows shift
across closed lids—
a silence
with shape

sap draws down
through the dark
slow and uncertain
as dreaming

Psalm 23

Coronary artery disease,
catheterization,
bypass, stent—

the words drip
from my doctor's mouth,
falling into the valley of shadow,

techné—
Your favored offspring
by my side.

Just keep walking,
I whisper,
through the valley
of shadow

Backyard Sutra

a flock of turkeys
fluttering—
such style!

one pauses—
tail a brushstroke,
head tilted, still

another struts
as if each step
were inked on rice paper

somewhere in the grass
the Buddha smiles—
a low chuckle,
nothing to teach

feathers rattle
in wind light—
the world bowing
to its own surprise

Praying on a Winter Day

The hush of freshly fallen snow
the silence of the God I seek
the loneliness of this forest home
on an icy winter day

the buzz of texts from far-off kids
who wish me well
the tofu and celery
in my wife's low-fat soup

the reel inside my mind
of when and how my doctor
will thread the tube
into my heart—and pause

the calcium, the pipes, the muscle
the machines, the stats, the stents
the faith in odds
and Pascal's wager, too

the reasoning mind exhausted,
the closing of my eyes,
the silence,
the prayer.

Lord Have Mercy

The pilgrimage to Santiago not taken
the Brie and the Gorgonzola not eaten

the arpeggios and arias never heard
the granddaughter's birthday not celebrated

the jog in Central Park delayed
the poem neither sung nor spoken

the widow maker wound around his heart
the tubes and stents inserted

Burma, Bengal, and Laos—
your tigers still roaming, still waiting

the train to Zermatt and Saas Fee empty
the old man alone in his bed

his films play quietly, again and again
his heart—still beating, still beating

his voice—still praying, still praying:
let me not be taken

Hallelujah

I wake from a fentanyl haze.
My cardiologist tells me I'm OK—
my pipes are patent,
blood flows to my heart
strong, silent, brave.

I emerge from the valley of shadow
onto the first light
of the rest of my life.

Energy bubbles up
through the arches of my feet.
A new space opens
between eyes and ears—
my forehead cool,
breath relaxed.
I recite Your name
as I inhale.

Why You listened to my prayers
I'll never know.
These steps I take
by the grace of a spirit
unseen, unknown.

Russian River, August 2024

dear redwoods
my great grandchildren
will they, too, touch you?

bark wide
as a grandfather's back
holding rain and shadow

roots braided
with ash fern stone—
the old stories quiet

sun climbs
your laddered spines
where spider light lingers

years pass
between rings
thicker than names

may their hands
find your heartwood
where mine rests now

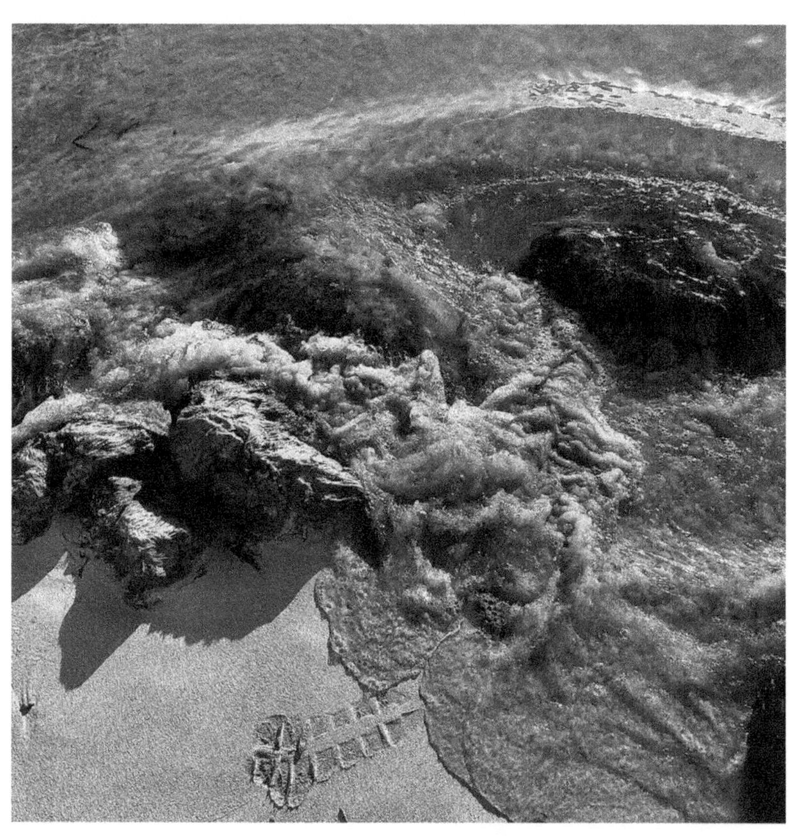

San Pedro, Belize, December 2024

the skies open—
the reef murmurs
through broken stone

ropes knock wood
under an idle dock

mangroves clutch
a rusted lighter,
crab shells,
a child's sock—
all held,
none sorted

I walk the shallows
glass chips underfoot

a bottle's mouth
filled with sand

rain comes sideways
across the flats

I close my eyes
as it falls
on all that drifts
and all that stays

Saint-Saëns's *The Swan* for Cello, July 2004

Allison draws her bow—
parting still water.

Notes glide
beneath her hands

through reeds
no eye can follow.

She leans into each phrase—
the curve of something passing.

I listen,
hands clasped,

my stillness—the shore
she traces with precision.

Church of Fog

A heron lifts
out of the river's mist—
white, like a breath you forget
was yours.

Nothing here is waiting.
The dew on the scalloped stone
does not ask
where you are from.

A bell swings once
in the absence of wind.
That's all.
I believe again.

Gjirokastër, Albania, November 2024

hands open
lines in her palms

an old lady begs
the call to prayer moans

her shawl, threadbare
holds the chill
of early dusk

no coins fall—
just footsteps
and pigeons scattering

her eyes closed
as if the earth itself
might answer

Syri i Kalter, Albania, November 2024

following her stream
cerulean tourmaline
my daughter—guiding me

watching her move
across the riverbed

dark limestone shifts
beneath her steps

my feet recede
with each stone she passes.

My Mother and the Tao

Light, swift, driven by the Tao,
flying through the winds of Acadia,
wandering with me
to the edge of an August beach
on the shores of Bar Harbor,
twenty years gone,
her spirit streaming
through the hollows of my mind.

My mother was born in Wisconsin in the late 1920s, into a Catholic family whose faith was as sturdy and spare as the Midwestern winters. She was raised on the rhythms of the liturgical calendar. Lent, Advent, Easter, and Christmas marked not just sacred time, but the domestic pulse of the household. Mass, confession, Marian devotions, and an unquestioning reverence for God shaped her early inner world. Yet even then, I believe, a quiet rebellion was forming. Not a rejection, but a questioning. A search for something purer, freer, lighter.

She moved east in her twenties and never returned to the Midwest to live, but the spaciousness of those childhood plains—open skies, long silences, golden fields—remained with her. She carried it into the apartments and houses she later made home.

My mother loved clean lines. Long after she moved to the Northeast, she recalled the cornfields and big skies of the Midwest and Great Plains with fondness. Her aesthetic was minimalist long before minimalism had a name: Brancusi, Klee, Zen gardens, the single line of a Basho haiku. She decluttered with the same devotion some reserve for prayer. "Less is more," she'd say, and I came to understand that this wasn't just about objects. It was about life and spirit, the aesthetics of spirituality—clean, simple, less—and the foundation of my eventual attraction to Buddhism and Taoism.

By the 1960s, amid the cultural upheavals that loosened so many from old certainties, my mother found Hermann Hesse. *Siddhartha* and *The Glass Bead Game* introduced her to a different conception of the sacred: not a God above, but a stillness within. Around the same time, she discovered Thomas Merton, first through his autobiography *The Seven Story Mountain*, then through his later, more contemplative writings. It was Merton's journey from Trappist silence into dialogue with Zen and Taoism that attracted her. In many ways, her own arc followed his: from Catholic discipline to mystic seeking.

And yet buried within her mid-twentieth century embrace of Buddhism and tai chi lay more than a kernel of childhood Catholicism. A triptych of Mother Mary hung by her bedside throughout her life. It was her link, I now think, to something unnameable: a mother of sorrows, a queen of compassion. In her later years, when I was old enough to wonder, I would sometimes ask her what she believed. She rarely answered directly. But the icon on the wall said everything: she hadn't forgotten. She hadn't let go.

She studied yoga when it was still considered esoteric and practiced tai chi years before it became mainstream. She once told me that it wasn't so much the movements she loved but the emptiness between them, the spaces, the pauses, the breaths. That was where she felt closest to God or the Tao, or whatever name she never insisted upon. Her devotion to the Alexander technique in the 1970s was also an extension of this impulse: aligning the body to release its habitual tensions, attuning awareness to balance and ease. This mind-body integration became, for her, a spiritual practice.

In later years, she gravitated more deeply toward Eastern philosophies. Zen, particularly its aesthetic, appealed to her, though I think she found its paradoxes unsettling. Taoism felt more natural to her temperament—fluid, yielding, unforced. She was never doctrinaire. She read Lao Tzu but didn't quote him. She moved through life the way water moves over stone. She never insisted I believe anything, but she opened doors, quietly. She left books out. Hesse, Merton, Alan Watts. When I was ready, I stepped through.

My earliest memories of my mother are infused with a kind of soft spiritual presence, rocking me lotus-style on her lap, humming Brahms, whispering lullabies that carried more peace than words. My mother was prone to depression, anxiety, and migraines, but my memories of her focus on her strengths. She was an early riser and an energetic lady. She always had a purpose in life and a plan for her day. A child of the Great Depression, she was thrifty and cautious with money in a way that Baby Boomers and Millennials might find puzzling. She was a nonconformist who never followed the crowd.

She was a perfectionist, especially when preparing for holidays. Her kitchen was sacred ground and not for children to mess up. Her eye for beauty infused every detail of family life, from table settings to Christmas carols. At Thanksgiving, Christmas, and Easter, we would gather at my parents' home in Connecticut and sit down at her dining room table. My mother spent days in advance preparing the table setting and cooking, making sure every object was clean and bright and in its proper place.

My mother loved art. As a young woman living on the Upper West Side of Manhattan in the 1950s, she attended evening art history courses at the Metropolitan Museum of Art. She would walk across Central Park in the dark (believe it or not, it was safe in those days) to attend lectures, and it was through her that I first learned about Romanesque and Gothic cathedrals, the Renaissance, Impressionism, and the work of Picasso, Klee, and Kandinsky. She dragged my sister and me to museums across Europe, and this early immersion led to my lifelong love of art and my preference for beauty in poetry and all things spiritual.

She majored in music, studied piano, and loved the cello, an instrument she gently placed in my hands and later into the hands of my children. She especially loved accompanying my daughter Allison on the cello. When Allison performed at her Suzuki recitals, my mother would play the piano beside her. I remember one recital in particular: her graduation from the Suzuki school in 2000. Allison played each note perfectly. We all beamed with pride, watching grandmother and granddaughter perform together, a sight as rare as it was precious.

She loved dawn. When I was a boy, she would take us to watch the sunrise over the Hudson River or from a mountain road in Europe, always chasing that first light. Once, when we lived in Tenafly, New Jersey, in the mid-1960s, she brought my sister Christina and me to the Palisades. I remember watching the fiery sun rise over the river, proud that we had caught the morning before anyone else had woken. That habit, the reverence for dawn, never left me.

Of course, there were storms too. As a teenager, I was reckless, rebellious—in short, a handful. I once shattered the glass of her Volvo station wagon in anger. And yet, no matter how turbulent things became, she always kept the door open. Her love was steady. When we both fell into depression during one of our family's sabbatical years in Switzerland, we shared an unspoken kinship in suffering. I sometimes wonder if my decision to become a psychiatrist had its roots in those early experiences of my mother's sadness and my own.

When I married Ninrong, my mother embraced her as both daughter and friend. Their bond, rooted in a shared love of gardening, music, clothes, and culture was a grace I never expected. And their connection planted deeper roots. I credit my mother with my choice of Ninrong, who grew up in China, as my wife. My mother's love of Asian art and culture had sparked my interest in Asia as a child and young adult. So, in a very real way, my children's mixed heritage owes much to her.

From 1997 to 2008, while we lived in Woodbridge, Connecticut, and before she passed away, I shared a particularly close bond with my mother, one shaped by music. I took up the cello again, and we played together often, especially Schumann, Beethoven, and Brahms. We even performed a Brahms cello sonata at a recital at the Neighborhood Music School in New Haven. Schumann's Adagio for cello and piano was our favorite. Whenever I hear its closing lines, mournful and romantic, I flash back to those years.

A family trip to Maui in 2006 stands out. Helicopter rides, luaus, walks on volcanic beaches, and an early morning drive to the summit of Haleakala. We searched for the sunrise but found only fog. A quiet parable, in retrospect.

Soon after that trip, she began to weaken. Back pain, fatigue, confusion. In August 2007, my father met me in the driveway, fear on his face. "Mama has lung cancer," he said. It didn't make sense. She had lived so purely, non-smoker, Alexander technique, tai chi. And yet, her life was unraveling. Between August and January, she declined. Oxygen tanks. ER visits. Moments of hope, then collapse.

Eventually, she was hospitalized. The prognosis was grim. I watched her body fail but saw her spirit still practicing. She breathed as best she could. She yielded. Morphine came. Hospice followed.

One night my father called. She had passed. I drove to the hospice, knelt beside her still body, and asked forgiveness. For what, I can't say. For all of it. For not loving her better. For not knowing.

It has taken me years to come to grips with my mother's passing. To this day, I feel her in my bones. I hope I get to see her someday, perhaps in Heaven, if such a place exists. I hope my children keep her memory alive in the years to come.

Her death changed me. But her spirit lives on in me. My return to Catholicism, with its mystical bent, is not a betrayal of her journey but a continuation. The Cloud of Unknowing. Pseudo-Dionysius. Merton, our shared pilgrim. And beside them, the Tao. Tai chi. Mindfulness. My mother taught me to dwell in stillness. To honor the breath. To find God not in thunder but in the silence after the rain. She lives in the spaces, just as she taught me.

THREE

REJOICING

Sunday, Near Bethesda Fountain, Central Park

No conductor.
Just a half-moon of bodies,
knees wide, palms raw,
a dozen drums arguing
like prophets—
interrupting, correcting,
praising.

One man's beat
stumbles, then stabs through,
splits the air
like glass cracking in heat.

Another leans into it—
a low belly-thump,
round as breath
held too long.

Someone adds
a rim tap,
off-time—
on purpose.

A woman smiles.
The rhythm shifts
like a flock mid-flight.

It's not music.
It's something older:
stone, skin,
bark peeled back to drum.
Worship without walls.

A call—
an answer—
missed,
caught,
returned.

Yuletide

Beam of winter solstice sun
slants across my son's cheeks,

notes of Bach he sings
across his cello strings,

this tender gift
on this darkest day,

sunlight on his face,
these melodies he plays,

sarabandes: slow voices
in the grain of wood,

courantes: quick steps
echoed in his touch,

allemandes: falterings
made graceful,

he rests his bow—
light remains.

Twelfth Night

Apples to apples
pick-up sticks,
Chinese checkers,
Christmas tricks

go tell it
on the mountain
by the crackling fire
the kids back home

the nutcrackers lined up—
the Buddha, the bodhisattvas,
the angels, the crèche,
the overeating, the naps

the holly, the yuletide log,
romcoms streaming,
nostalgic shows—
the Tin Man, the Scarecrow,
and the Lion, too

when the bobcat and the deer
wander by the old stone wall,
and the black bear hibernates
beneath brush pile sheets

lazy, silly, and complete—
our fingers guiding marbles
across the board,
picking up sticks from the floor

hopping and jumping
and dancing all night,
falling asleep once more.

Forest Games

acorns on our heads
raining down—
we freeze,
as if the forest
is deciding something

one bounces
off your shoulder

another lands
in my hood—
I keep it
like a prayer

Soup Kitchen Prayer

bless these juicy meatballs,
the lasagna, the endless trays of roasted chicken,
the multi-colored carrots,
the carbs,
the oceans of mashed potatoes,
and that red sauce stuck to the bottom of the pan

may You flow
through our hands and backs and arms,
through our feet,
uniting those who serve,
those who eat,
those who shuffle,
those who speak,

and especially those who shout,
the troublemakers,
the prophets—
who wake us from our slumber
and stir our doubt,

all of us gathered,
one breath,
here with You,
now.

Offerings to the Exercise Gods

The high priestess of spin
at her altar of chrome
calls us to worship
on New Year's Eve.

Led Zeppelin roars—
diehards, converts, true believers—
we offer speed and sweat.

Defying Lady Fortune
and the spokes of her wheel,
we chant our creed:

good works of strength and cardio
will ward off old age,
heart disease, stroke, even death.

Endorphins flood the nave.
The priestess gives communion:
bran muffins and virgin mimosas.

We imbibe,
we merge
hearts beating—
one last amen

Union Square Market, Saturday

whiff of cilantro—
a breeze from Chao Phraya
threads between the stalls

basil wilts
in the canvas fold,
rain darkening my sandals

galangal curls—
a vendor laughs—
lime leaves torn open
like old paper

lemongrass crossed,
at the bottom of the crate,
tamarind scent
rising with the steam

I lift one root—
the market hum recedes—
turmeric left
like memory on my skin

Smiling on a Winter Day

On steely winter days
when leafless branches
point to a blue-gray sky
like the arms of the dead,

and God makes Herself scarce—
so scarce I wonder
if She's still there—

on late January afternoons
when friends in Arizona
send photos from the basketball court,
shirts off in the sun,

I turn away,
close my eyes,
and think of you—

your voice, your hands,
your laugh, your mind,
your noodles, your dumplings,
a hot cup of green tea.

And just for a moment
I let myself smile.

Fugue at Daybreak

last dreams fade
the orchestra plays its first notes
blackbird robin jay

blackbird begins—
three notes, spaced wide
like footsteps
in dew-soaked grass

robin follows
from the fence's spine—
same shape,
slightly altered in the throat

then jay—
a burst of cobalt
breaking the pattern
but not the thread

the fugue unfolds
through branch, wire, eave,
each voice settling
inside the next—

I listen, barefoot
on the morning earth—
as if I'd stepped
into a prayer.

Orangutan Meets Heidegger,
Tanjung Puting, Borneo, Indonesia, 2025

She moves through humid light
as through old film,
green spooling over rust,
shadows flicker on rattan.

Her face, creased, unhurried,
settles into calm,
needing no thought,
only the weight of seeing.

We share a frame,
twelve million years

apart,
until the leaves
claim her shape again.

Bornean Clouded Leopard,
Night Along the Sekonyer, October 2025

The flashlight finds her,
moving through rain gloss,
palm trunks, broken roots.

She halts, one paw lifted,
eyes fixed in the beam,
still as rain.

I feel her watching,
the quiet between us
pressed by heat.

For a moment,
I believe we share it,
her beauty, her doubt,
her wish to vanish.

Then she moves,
her coat dissolving
in the rain's small noise.

Incarnation

cottonwood puffs
rising in the air—
winged beings

one lands
then loosens
from my sleeve

no weight, no message—
yet I turn
as if someone
had spoken my name

the air empties
nothing to hold
only this brief belonging

Chestnut and Bamboo,
Woodbridge, Connecticut, Winter 2024

1.

Today I threw out our money tree.
Malabar Chestnut of twenty-seven years,
braided trunk, sturdy, glossy leaves,
green through all the leanest winters.

Money isn't often mentioned in poems.
More taboo than sex,
and harder to make beautiful.
Still, this tree earned its place.

It paid off our home,
sent the kids to college,
even granted a few trips
to the far corners of the world.

It added up, in its quiet way.

But now my wife insists—
a strange conviction in her voice—
it must go.
And she never tells me to throw things out.

So, I did.

Lifted it by the base,
steadying the neck of its braided trunk,
carried it out behind the house
to the low stone wall.
Tipped the pot,
shook it loose,

laid it gently down
on a bed of brittle brush.

Winter sky, pale red and yellow.
Leaves curled like old receipts.
No ceremony.
Just silence.

2.

I stepped back inside.

In its place—already—
a new presence.
Lucky bamboo.

Five slender stalks,
banded and green,
looped with a red velvet ribbon
like a gift that knew it would be opened.

Now that we're older,
my wife explained,
it's no longer right
to wish for more than we need.

So, we've traded abundance
for health.
A softer form of hope.

No strokes, no falls, no sudden collapse—
we don't say these things aloud.
But we water the stalks each week,
speak gently in their presence.

A happy tree.
A smiling Buddha.
That might be enough.

Roadside Banquet

acorns crushed on the road—
nature's smoothie

squirrels dash through leaves
sampling the mix

ants trace spirals—
no menu, no complaint

a jay drops in
beak tipped in pulp

the wind stirs
what's left in the crack—

as if nothing
goes unnoticed

Water Falling

legs, lines
kisses on our eyes
seared across years

returning to this clearing
your hands finding mine

across dandelions, knotweed nettles,
wild raspberries,
beds of broken birch bark,

waterfalls spraying,
glint of minnow pools

fog lifting
our breaths mingling—
vows unfolding

Words and Pictures

Eyes entrained
to cancer,
nuclei in nasty moods,
you, the pathologist,

swimming in seas of cells,
I, the psychiatrist, in words.
What a match,
our quarrels

money, kids, politics,
I preferring
"yes" or "no,"
your comfort in the flow,

my strings of syllables
melt beneath your gaze,
your eurekas of discovery,
I-Spy passions

dissolve my words,
those symbols I revered
subsumed in puzzle pieces
fitted by your quiet hands
across the years.

Let Not Your Hearts Be Troubled

this morning again
the hydrangeas sway—

their heads nodding—
yes, yes, everything's OK

a breeze, or maybe
something they believe

I stand a while
pretending to sip my tea—

no verses come
but still, they speak—

each bloom
a quiet assurance

they keep swaying
as if they know
what I keep forgetting

FOUR

ACCEPTING

My Father

In Te, Domine Speravi

This essay explores the spiritual legacy of my father, a man of science and silence, shaped by war and wonder, whose unspoken reverence for life has shaped my own journey toward the sacred. While he rarely spoke in religious terms, his life embodied the quiet theology of attention, awe, and love.

Several years before my father passed away, he asked that the words *In Te, Domine Speravi* be inscribed on his gravestone. When I asked what the Latin meant, he replied, "In you, Lord, I have hoped." His answer left a lasting impression. It was more than a final wish. It was a distillation of his spiritual orientation: quiet, probing, tentative, but deeply felt. That simple phrase now seems to me like the seed of a theology, not an expression of certainty, but of existential trust.

My father was a rigorous natural scientist, a man of empirical discipline and data, yet he always left the door open to the mystery of God, not a God of systems or dogma, but a presence that listened and responded, however silently. Without such a God, he once told me, there could be no real hope. That was why he chose *In Te, Domine Speravi:* because he hoped that such a God might exist. It was a wager of the heart, not the intellect, a longing held in tension with his agnosticism. And in that tension, his life acquired a devotional quality, not through doctrine, but through moral seriousness.

His spirituality flowed through his life like a hidden current, rarely named, seldom discussed, yet everywhere present. He carried within him a quiet awe: for the elegance of the natural world, the mystery of Christ, and the moral conundrum of suffering. Like Tolstoy, Dostoevsky, and Bonhoeffer, he sensed that if God existed,

He was no remote clockmaker, but something closer, intimately bound to human suffering. And yet, my father remained metaphysically modest. He distrusted proclamations. He believed that truth revealed itself through the life well lived. In retrospect, his was a kind of lay mysticism, stripped of ritual, but rooted in reverence. He embodied Pascal's insight that "the heart has its reasons, which reason knows nothing of."

Science, he insisted, could not answer the questions that mattered most: how to live, why we love, what beauty means. Though his career advanced through the rigor of experimental physiology, he never confused scientific precision with spiritual understanding. These two realms, rational inquiry and existential yearning, coexisted within him in paradoxical harmony. In this, I now see the essential shape of his spirituality: an embrace of tension, a refusal of easy answers, a contemplative posture before mystery. His stance was one of detachment, of learning to dwell in unknowing.

That acceptance reminds me of Kierkegaard's view that faith begins where reason ends, not because faith is irrational, but because it moves within a domain that reason cannot fully chart. Like Kierkegaard's knight of faith, my father moved quietly through the ordinary world, trusting in what could not be proven.

His life was also a story of rupture and reinvention. Born in wartime Vienna, he came of age surrounded by ideological extremism and violence. From the swastika to Soviet tanks, his youth was shaped by forces that shattered certainties. And yet he emerged neither bitter nor cynical. Instead, he found consolation in music, in history, in the mountains. These became his sacred texts, the places where his spirit found its clearest expression.

My father rarely spoke about spiritual matters, but I believe he lived his faith, not a faith of creeds, but of witness. He believed in the value of small acts, quiet truths, and honest questions. His childhood was shaped by trauma and instability, and he seemed to emerge from it with the belief that meaning must be sought, not assumed. That search became a kind of spiritual discipline.

Even his intellectual humility had a spiritual dimension. He never claimed to have final answers, not even in science. "Never trust the one who claims to know," he once told me. "Ask instead: what kind of life do they live?"

Who was my father, and how did my relationship with him shape my relationship with God? How did his spiritual temperament influence my faith?

As a boy, I experienced my father as larger than life. I revered him and sought to emulate him. As an adolescent and young adult, I rejected him, only to return. As a parent and physician, I built an identity separate from his. As he aged and grew frail, I became his caregiver. And now that he is gone, I carry forward many of his passions and values. To this day, he remains a living presence within me.

As a child and young adult, I failed to grasp the immensity of the transformation my father underwent, immigrating from Austria to America. He came from a world utterly unlike the one in which he would eventually raise my sister and me.

Just imagine the distance he traveled between 1943 and 1963. In 1943, he was a teenager in Nazi-occupied Vienna, practicing piano in a crumbling apartment, his parents barely able to feed him. Twenty years later, he was a US citizen living in a New Jersey split-level with a Rambler station wagon, a lawn to mow, and a faculty position at Cornell. He flew in jets, lectured in English, and lived in a land of freedom and consumer abundance.

By contrast, my own life has been stable. Twenty years ago, I lived in the same house where I live today. Though the internet and the pandemic have reshaped the cultural landscape, the underlying structure of my life has remained constant. Not so for my father. His capacity to survive and flourish is something I only began to appreciate in middle age.

By 1968, just sixteen years after arriving in the US, he had become chair of the department of physiology at Yale and held an endowed professorship. It's hard not to compare: what had I accomplished by age forty-one? My father was a giant. I've spent much of my life trying to emerge from beneath his shadow.

He embodied a remarkable constellation of traits, at once shy and modest, ambitious and competitive, scientific and spiritual.

Though his professional life centered on science and technology, he was equally drawn to history, philosophy, music, and art. He climbed mountains and attended operas. He read voraciously. His intellectual curiosity was not simply academic. It was a way of seeking meaning.

Leafing through his diaries, kept from 1966 through the early 2010s, before dementia intervened, I'm amazed at how much he packed into each day. He met with colleagues, attended NIH committees in DC, hosted mid-week cocktail parties, shuttled me to swimming and cello lessons, and wrote weekly letters to his mother in Austria, all while reading European history and Russian fiction, and squeezing in work trips to Europe, Asia, and South America.

My mother used to joke that he had a "love affair with the kidney." He was a scientist's scientist, dedicated to understanding physiology at its most fundamental level. He believed in knowledge for its own sake. He published hundreds of papers, coauthored numerous textbooks, and trained over sixty postdoctoral fellows, many of whom went on to lead departments worldwide. He won countless awards and, in the early 1970s, was nominated for the Nobel Prize.

When I was young, my mother explained that scientists in our age were the equivalent of Renaissance artists, people driven by vision and devotion to beauty and truth. I believe she was right. Living with my father was like living with an artist, someone who gave himself wholly to a calling. Science was his sacred obsession.

It often came first. I struggled to gain his attention, to share mental and emotional shelf space with his work. I spent years trying to earn my place in his world.

What was it like growing up with such a father? As a child, I felt proud. He inhabited a realm that was rarefied and mysterious. Later, I entered medical school, partly because I wanted to access that world.

My earliest memories are of him climbing over boulders with my sister and me in Fort Tryon Park in Manhattan. In hindsight, these felt like rituals, liturgies of observation and companionship.

My father loved mountains. Years later, we would hike the Italian Dolomites and the Swiss Alps. My father had an adventurous streak. By the summer of 1970, he would take me up the Amazon River. Beneath his quiet demeanor lived an explorer.

But a traumatized one. I can only imagine what he witnessed growing up. American planes strafed him and his father with machine-gun fire as they ran for cover. Russian troops with flamethrowers pursued him and his friend Fritz on the outskirts of Vienna. He saw deserters hanged from trees. He watched Soviet troops loot his home. His silence about those years wasn't mere reticence. It was reverence. He had seen the abyss and chose, quietly, to live toward the light.

He didn't volunteer these stories. His attention was rooted in the present. He smiled rarely, and even his greatest joys were shaded by melancholy. As an only child, he bore guilt for leaving his widowed mother in Austria. He wrote her hundreds of letters. And though he lived in America for over six decades, he never fully acclimated. A part of him always remained elsewhere.

Behind the accolades lay intense discipline. He once told me, "Many scientists have good ideas. The great ones act on them." So, he worked weekends. After we moved to New Jersey in 1963, he brought me with him on Saturdays to his lab on East 69th Street in Manhattan. He wore a white coat and typed research papers. I sat across from him, drawing castles and people on yellow lined paper. I was six or seven. Only later did I realize that those years were the height of his creative output. Looking back, I see not only discipline, but a kind of spiritual order, a life structured in answer to chaos.

Of course, I remember his absences. He traveled constantly—Washington, Tokyo, Paris, London, Munich, Zurich, São Paulo, Caracas. Immediately after we moved to Connecticut in 1968, he left for Europe for two months. My sister and I crawled into our mother's bed at night. He returned weeks later with stories, photographs, and gifts.

He didn't just travel. He uprooted us. We moved from New Jersey to Bern, then back to New Jersey, then to Connecticut, São Paulo, Connecticut again, then Geneva. Throughout elementary and high school, I was constantly starting over—new friends, new languages, new schools. I struggled in Swiss public school, taught in German, and spent my early teens fearing another transatlantic move. My father nearly accepted a professorship in Switzerland. I studied German fervently, just in case.

As a child, I resented the instability. Science came first, and we were expected to follow. I complained and blamed him. Only later did I recognize the richness of those years abroad. As a child, I chafed; as an adult, I remain grateful.

As I entered adolescence, I rebelled against my father. I smoked marijuana, rejected classical music in favor of Jimi Hendrix, and argued with him about politics. America and capitalism were bad, Marxism and socialism, good. Most of all, his generation didn't see the world the way we did. They called it "The Generation Gap," and in my case, it was compounded by a deeper feeling, true to some extent, that my father didn't understand what it meant to grow up in America. He listened to opera, didn't follow sports, and seemed out of step with the culture around me. That made me feel different from other kids, just when I most wanted to fit in.

I stayed out late, had an affair with an older woman, and tested my father's patience. I was moody, angry, depressed, and unpredictable. I pushed him away. To this day, I regret the way I treated him. He had grown up in Austria, shaped by poverty and war. And there I was, a spoiled American teenager, convinced I had all the answers.

I remember once arguing with him at the kitchen table. I wanted to buy tickets to see Elton John in New Haven. My parents thought I was too young, and since I was only in eighth grade, they were probably right. My father grew so frustrated that he threw a cup of water in my face.

Otherwise, he was an extraordinarily gentle man. He rarely scolded me or raised his voice. I don't recall ever having a formal conversation with him about "right and wrong." He led by quiet example. He spoke generously of his colleagues and students, never criticized others, and projected humility. Privately, he confided to me his own anxieties about being a foreign-born academic in a world of professors educated at elite American institutions. He had missed much of high school during World War II and entered medical school in Vienna as one of thousands. His education had been anything but privileged.

Even at the height of our conflicts, we shared many magical moments. I recall playing ping pong with him in our basement in suburban New Jersey; hiking with him in Connecticut in the late sixties and early seventies; and walking with him in the Swiss Alps. In 1989 we hiked the *haute route* from Chamonix to Zermatt.

We spent countless evenings in our basement darkroom, developing black-and-white photos of the Italian Dolomites, "burning in" clouds and sharpening mountain ridgelines. In 1970 we traveled up the Amazon into the Brazilian jungle. These were unforgettable journeys, literal and emotional, that stitched our lives together more than either of us could articulate at the time.

And then there was all the culture. From an early age, I learned to relate to my father through history, literature, and classical music. From him, I inherited a lifelong passion for learning and for beauty. Our home was filled with the music of Bach, Telemann, Vivaldi, Haydn, Mozart, Beethoven, Schumann, Chopin, Mahler, and Brahms. It was that music that eventually led me to the cello. He also ignited my love of history, which began with Europe and expanded to Asia. Culture was always the open door to my father's heart.

There were times when I wished that door included popular culture, sports, and card games. As a teenager, I once chided him for wanting our lives to run "as smoothly as a Mozart symphony," an especially cutting remark since Mozart was Austrian, and my father adored him. In time, I came to understand that he was never meant to be an "all-American dad." He was my Papa, a European intellectual who read Tolstoy, Camus, and Dostoevsky, who spent a lifetime as an autodidact, always learning French, reading another book, attending an opera, or visiting a museum.

Despite his accomplishments, my father was a shy man. I remember once coming home from Harvard and driving with him to his office at Yale. We exited his Volvo in the parking lot, and when he saw a professor who intimidated him, he quietly led us round a building to avoid being seen. That moment stayed with me. It revealed something tender and uncertain beneath the surface of his authority.

In college I formed my own identity, studying history, applying to law school, only to pivot at the last moment and follow his path into medicine. I became a psychiatrist, carving out my own niche. And then I returned to Connecticut to raise a family, perhaps like a salmon swimming upstream to its source. I believe that arc—back to medicine, to Connecticut, and ultimately to faith—was shaped, however unconsciously, by the example of my father.

Even after spending more than two decades away from Connecticut, living in Cambridge, San Francisco, Palo Alto, Philadelphia, and New York, I returned to live near my father. Why? Because I wanted to be close to him, to share time with him, and above all, because I wanted my children to know him. By my late thirties, I had come to respect my father. I recognized that he was a great man.

Once I settled into private practice and began raising our children, my relationship with my father changed. The old traces of adolescent rebellion faded. In my forties, as he entered his seventies, I came to treasure our time together. We shared books, especially philosophy, which had become a growing passion of his later in life. He inspired me to read Plato's *Dialogues*, Aristotle's *Ethics*, Kant's *Critique of Pure Reason*, and Heidegger's *Being and Time*. He loved discussing Karl Popper, Ludwig Wittgenstein, Blaise Pascal, and Søren Kierkegaard. Like me, he was a seeker, drawn to the Greek Stoics, especially the emperor Marcus Aurelius, the emancipated slave Epictetus, and the aristocrat Seneca.

I cherished those years of sharing ideas with him. From my father, I inherited a learned ignorance, a kind of metaphysical humility. The more he knew, the more he appreciated the limits of knowledge. As he aged, he would remind me that the hard sciences to which he had devoted his life offered little guidance on the deeper questions: why we are here, and how we should live.

A quiet awareness of the mystery of God always accompanied

him. He held a deep respect for mystical thinkers like Meister Eckhart. Our conversations about philosophy became, for me, a kind of spiritual formation. He was not a believer in the traditional sense, but his pursuit of wisdom had the gravity and reverence of prayer.

Although my father read philosophy and theology voraciously, what moved me most was his gentleness and generosity. When he saw someone begging on the streets of New Haven, he would pull over, reach into his pocket, and hand them several dollars. He was immune to arguments that such kindness encouraged dependency. Having grown up amid the poverty of mid-twentieth-century Central Europe, he recognized human need when he saw it.

Likewise, despite, or perhaps because of, his years conducting medical research on animals, he became deeply sensitive to their suffering. In the 1960s, when my sister and I were children, he brought home rabbits, gerbils, and guinea pigs rescued, I now realize, from his lab. Years later, he confided that he had performed experiments on dogs, frogs, and rats. He felt genuine remorse. In his later years, he took care never to harm any living creature. He fed stray cats, gently relocated crickets and spiders from the house to the backyard and treated all sentient beings with quiet reverence. He didn't need to be Buddhist or Hindu to live out their ethic of compassion.

Only now do I realize how rarely we discussed religion, especially organized religion. His spiritual lineage was complex. His maternal grandfather was Jewish. His father, born Catholic, converted to Protestantism after a divorce following the First World War. My father thus grew up Protestant in an overwhelmingly Catholic Austria. Perhaps for that reason, he gave little weight to denominational divisions. What mattered to him was Christ as the suffering servant, the advocate of the poor and oppressed.

As a lifelong student of European history, he was keenly aware of the horrors wrought by religious violence, especially the Thirty Years War. Having survived Nazism as a youth and the Soviet occupation of Vienna after World War II, he viewed all ideological extremism, secular or religious, with deep suspicion. He embraced

Enlightenment ideals of tolerance and respect for differing viewpoints. As a natural scientist, he rejected creationism and all forms of religious fundamentalism. I internalized these values.

In his later years, my father often spoke of Eckhart's idea of the "divine spark" in every soul. Like the Buddhist notion of Buddha-nature, it echoed a deep intuition of his, that something sacred dwells in all that lives. He never framed this belief dogmatically, but I believe it quietly guided his conduct. Eckhart taught that the path to God requires letting go of God as a concept or an image to allow the divine to be born in the soul. My father, too, approached God not by grasping but by releasing: releasing ego, certainties, and the need for final answers.

But all of this leads to a deeper question: What, truly, did my father believe? His bookshelf offered clues—Pascal, Kierkegaard, Eckhart, Tolstoy—but his life revealed more. Beyond science, it was love that formed the axis around which his spiritual world revolved. My father believed in the quiet power of love, and through his deep attachment to family, he practiced that belief, less as a creed than as lived conviction.

As our children grew, my father entered a kind of golden age, those years from the late 1990s until 2008, when all three generations coexisted under a shared roof of affection and continuity. He adored his grandchildren, took special delight in teaching them German, listening to their cello practice, and, most memorably, traveling with them to Maui in the summer of 2006.

In 2002, on a series of quiet Sunday afternoons, I sat with him and read my grandfather's poems out loud in German. We tried to translate them into English. I asked him about our ancestors. I felt a growing urgency to preserve their stories, to keep something of them alive before it slipped away. These people from Moravia, Austria, Germany, and Poland had lived through upheavals that still echoed. My father shared some memories, though he seemed less drawn to the past than I was, perhaps because so much of it was marked by trauma.

He didn't romanticize our forebears. Nor was he especially interested in their religious or spiritual lives. They had emerged from the school of hard knocks, survivors of the turmoil that defined early- and mid-twentieth-century Central Europe. Still, I believe his awareness of their collective suffering shaped his spirituality. That kind of suffering cried out for the existence of a benevolent God, even if the historical facts made such belief feel, at times, almost absurd.

In 2007, my relationship with my father changed forever. My mother's sudden diagnosis and death from lung cancer upended his life. Just a few years earlier, he had retired from Yale. Now, with both his spouse and career gone, he struggled to find his bearings. He had long relied on my mother to manage the household, oversee their finances, and maintain their social ties. When she was gone, all of it unraveled. I had always assumed my father would be the first to go. But life didn't follow the script.

He once confided that he had always feared something terrible might happen to him later in life. My mother's illness was that moment. He watched helplessly as she held on through her final months. As death approached, he wrestled with guilt for not having said "I love you" often enough, for not having done more.

After my mother died, my father entered a sort of spiritual winter. Their marriage had lasted over half a century. She had been his companion in the deepest sense, grounding his restless intellect. Her death unsettled him not just emotionally but existentially. In its wake, I saw a vulnerability in him I had never witnessed before. He spoke more openly of his fears and regrets. And he began to express a quiet longing for belonging, for ritual, for something eternal. Her absence left not just a human void, but a theological one, a rupture that opened larger questions about meaning, presence, and the afterlife.

His philosophical restraint shaped the way he bore suffering. After my mother's death, something in him collapsed. He became physically and emotionally diminished. Yet in that collapse, something was revealed. He did not respond with denial or anger, but with sorrow and then with silence. And in that silence, a kind of grace.

He told me once that he had always wanted to receive the Catholic Mass. "I wish I could believe fully," he said. "I wish I could feel at home in a church." That longing was a kind of prayer. I believe that my own later embrace of Catholicism was, in part, a way of stepping toward him or meeting him in a place he could never fully enter.

I recall the quiet mornings we spent together. He would sit at the breakfast table without speaking, gazing at the shifting light on the wall. Late winter afternoons were hardest. He lost track of time, forgot to pay bills, and fell prey to telephone scams. Friends and colleagues drifted away. His social world withered.

Our roles reversed. My father grew dependent on my sister and me. I managed his finances and tended to the mechanics of his life—medications, mail, appointments, television, internet, lawn, driveway. Eventually, I took away the keys to his Porsche and his Volvo. I arranged for live-in care.

He had lived such a vigorous life, so intellectually sharp, that watching my father's decline felt all the more cruel. I reached out to his colleagues to explain that he was no longer able to travel or speak publicly. He could still discuss French politics or the Habsburgs, but he no longer remembered what day it was or what he'd eaten for breakfast. I saw, in his fading, a glimpse of my own future. His world narrowed. His sense of time and place disintegrated. The lesson was stark: no matter how luminous a life may be, the same fate awaits us all—old age, frailty, sickness, and death.

I often wondered what my father believed as he approached the end. I never fully found out. He had studied theology, but whether he believed in an afterlife remained unclear. Like many intellectuals, he likely remained quietly agnostic. But I do know this: he believed deeply in love and kindness. He always felt for the poor, for those he called "broken wings," people who had failed to find happiness. He understood suffering as central to the Christ story. And, in time, he seemed to accept it as central to his own.

Even as dementia silenced most of his speech, his gestures remained eloquent. He still fed the birds. He still gazed with quiet awe at the snow falling through the pines outside his window. He reached for my hand. These were his final prayers.

In January 2019 a vicious ice storm hit Connecticut. Temperatures plunged below zero Fahrenheit. The pipes in my father's home froze and broke. He lost power and telephone service. He sat alone with his live-in helper, whose mobile phone didn't work. I knew I must do something to save him.

I jumped into my Acura, navigated the icy hills of Woodbridge, and arrived to find a fallen tree blocking his driveway. I parked on the street, hiked over the ice-crusted snow, and rang the doorbell. His helper emerged from the dark and let me in. I called the police and fire department, but they were of no use. The driveway was impassable. So, I placed my father in a wheelchair, pushed him across the ice, and loaded him into my car. He spent the next couple of weeks at our home until I could restore power, heat, and water to his.

From that day on, I knew I must live on call, waiting for the next disaster to strike. And it did. Over the following year, my father endured several bouts of pneumonia from which he never recovered. He lost his appetite, his will to live, and slowly wasted away. My sister brought him childhood picture books—one I remember featured Robinson Crusoe—to help him pass the time.

In April 2020, at 5:00 a.m., a doctor called to tell me my father had been admitted to the hospital. He tested negative for COVID, was transferred to a hospice, and died there a few days later.

I arrived at his bedside a couple of hours after he passed. His hands were folded, as if in supplication. It felt like a final statement. He had lived with restraint, with reverence, with responsibility. He had lived according to a question: What does it mean to be human in a world of mystery? I sat beside him, filled with both sorrow and a strange peace. In that moment, it seemed he had lived exactly as he had believed, with an open door to the divine.

In the years since my father's passing, my life has taken on an uncanny resemblance to his. During the pandemic lockdown, I read the Western Canon he had cherished, including novels by Dostoyevsky and Tolstoy and European histories he had gifted me. I returned to the Metropolitan Museum of Art in New York and studied the Renaissance artists and Dutch Masters he revered. I visited Florence, the home of the Medici, a city he had always urged me to see.

I listened to Bach, Handel, Mozart, Haydn, and Beethoven, the composers he had worshiped. I made pilgrimages to Vienna and to Weikertschlag, my grandfather's ancestral village on the Austrian-Czech border.

With my father's death, I felt free to embrace him. I no longer needed to be different from him to be free.

Now that he is gone, when I listen to Bach, I feel as if he is speaking to me. When I see a mountain peak, a quiet path through the forest, or a piece of architecture that lifts the spirit, I sense his presence. His modesty, his intellectual honesty, his generosity, his kindness—these are qualities to which I aspire.

My father rarely spoke of God, but his reverence for life was unmistakable. I remember him pausing before a glacial peak or an alpine flower with the same solemnity one brings to prayer. He found the divine not in doctrine but in detail, the curve of a Gothic arch, the phrasing of a Bach fugue, the intricacy of the human body. His sense of the sacred was always rooted in the particular. As Meister Eckhart might have said, God is born in the soul in the act of attention.

My father embodied a sort of spiritual integrity that transcended belief. My journey through Buddhism and later into the Catholic mystical tradition would not have unfolded without the quiet template of his spiritual temperament. He helped me understand that religious identity is not a fixed creed, but a posture toward the mystery of existence.

His was not a spirituality of answers, but of attentiveness. He paid close attention to the world. And in doing so, he practiced a kind of lay devotion. I saw it in his kindness to the poor, his remorse over animal suffering, and the letters he wrote to his aging mother. These were sacraments of a different order, embodied expressions of a faith that required no formal declaration.

My father never claimed to know the mind of God. But he trusted that it was worth seeking. *In Te, Domine Speravi.* In you, Lord, I have hoped.

Christ in Linden

I stand alone,
shadow bent across the chapel floor.

They said it was linden—
soft wood, light grained.

The folds ripple
as if they move.

The robe he wears—
the carver knew

how fabric falls
once breath has left.

In the hollows,
the cloth remembers

a silence still breathing

Flushing, Queens

holding your hand
wading through Chinatown
an old man plays *erhu*

fish shimmer on ice
steam curls from pork buns
a woman sings to herself

your fingers tighten
at a crosswalk—
then slip back into mine

San Francisco

bags packed
the dawn star fades—
homesick at the door

a silver pin
above the Mission hills—
last to vanish
before the light takes hold

I watch it tremble
in the bay wind,
as if deciding
what to bless, what to keep

fog presses in—
breath held
between two hearts

one turning east,
the other
still listening

Gazing out My Window

Enclosed,
bathed in winter light—
my heart aching

this bird in me lifts
over the Hudson,
past freight yards, low clouds—
Montana, Idaho—
the air thins

Honolulu, Shanghai—
cities I barely touch—
past old Borobudur,
Angkor Wat in silence,
and the Shwedagon,
gold flaring against dusk

over the Bay of Bengal,
the Himalayas breathing below,
the great Central Asian plateau
folding into shadow

Vienna recedes,
London flickers—

and before I know
I'm back home—
gazing out this window
in my room

a mansion in the forest,
a box in the sky—
does it matter
where I lie?

Climate Blues

A driveway shining wet,
rain ticking on a windowsill,
a moth against the glass—
wings too thin for February—
and I, reaching toward what's gone.

My winter coat in the hallway?
The kids' rusted sled in the garage?
A scarf, plaid and pilled,
folded soft in a drawer—
my mother's last gift.

I open the door.
A warm wind, low and dense,
slips past my collar.
Geese call overhead,
circling, not departing.

Bare branches, still,
yet tipped with restless buds—
tight-fisted, waiting.

A single mosquito wanders,
its path uncertain.

I close my eyes.
The hush of snow returns—
the crackle underfoot,
the laughter rolling downhill,
the blur of red plastic.

I zip my coat—
some things
I still pretend.

Inshallah

Inshallah,

I will meet you someday,
on the other side of tomorrow—
your eyes, your lips,
your hands, your breath, your smile.

Inshallah,

reaching back
to the Yellow River valley,
the Danube, the fields of Moravia,
the paddies of the Yangtze, too.

Inshallah,

I will dream of you, little one—
hold you in my arms,
afraid my hands might tremble
before I place you in my daughter's.

Inshallah,

I will hobble with a cane,
bent and shuffling with my years,
smiling my quiet smile,
your image flickering in my mind.

Inshallah,

I will coo and babble to you,
mirror your voice
before the world crowds in
with names and rules.

Inshallah,

I will pray for you
as the sun folds
into the winter sky—
alone, but never alone.

Inshallah,

you are the reason why.

Sages

Chinese silver grass
reaching old age
six, seven feet tall

conferring in the wind
nodding slightly
long pauses

some lean closer
then return
to their stance

none speaks first
none resist
what passes through

Methuselah

the crowns of the old oaks
catch their last rays
cloaked in gray

evening birds
don't sing
they just settle

the forest sleeps
tree by tree
whispering into dreams

By My Mother's Grave

planting August mums
dreaming autumn blossoms
dirt beneath my nails

a beetle turns
in the shade of the stone—
I let it be

roots won't take
where she lies—
I try again

wind lifts
a torn tag
from the plastic pot

Far Away

Tai chi in the park
floating in mist
my wife—in Nanjing

my arms follow air
vanish in gray

her name
rests in the breath
that stays with me

a sparrow lifts
from the wet railing—
its wings don't ask the distance

I turn with the form,
palm to sky,
as if the clouds might answer

a crack in the pavement
holds yesterday's rain—
still, reflecting

a shape in the fog
almost her—
but it passes

my hands return
to stillness—

held
by what's unseen

On Attending Jon's Memorial or Petals Falling

The tears I shed
welling up
streaming down my face

the hands we shook
the petals of remembrance
we placed in your vase

the genealogies you constructed
Genghis Khan, Jesus, King Arthur
tenuously related to you and me

the pictures you painted
of planets, spaceships, aliens
tethered to us on Mother Earth

the wisdom of your madness
that we are all brothers
linked by blood across the ages

Komodo Dragon Tour, Indonesia

Halfway around the world
for dragons.
A narrow trail,
scrub trees,
heat like a wall.

A ranger with a stick
points to one,
a gray body in the dust,
motionless,
breathing slowly.

Tourists circle,
phones raised,
the air smelling of salt and diesel.

So this is it,
I think,
the myth reduced
to a lizard
in the sun.

And still,
something ancient stirs,
the way its tongue flicks,
the way it doesn't care
we've come so far.

Old Man Monk, Burma, January 2006

To give up his home,
his money, his name—

to step into the street
and walk away,

sticky rice, papaya slice
drop into his bowl,

his working days behind him,
jasmine in the air—

an old man begging
on the road to Mandalay.

Queens Bound, 14th Street, January 6, 2024

He boarded at 14th
with a duffel—military-issue, frayed strap.
His hand
tapping once
against his thigh,
then still.

Stood swaying—
one hand on the pole,
the other clutching
a hospital cup,
rattling with change.

The car shifted—
no one looked.

A woman in scrubs,
stethoscope coiled in her coat pocket,
unearthed a clementine
from between an inhaler
and an energy bar
and held it out.
He took it
like it weighed something—
like it might bruise.

He didn't speak.
She didn't ask.

The train rose
at Queensboro Plaza—
a slant of winter light
cut across
his wrist,
its skin pocked
with old track marks.

She was already gone.
So was he.

In the air,
the scent of citrus.

On Visiting Borobudur, Java, October 2025

Bells of andesite
rise tier on tier,

seventy-two hollows,
stone within light.

Beneath them, hundreds more
endure the heat.

I move among them,
a body between bells.

Walking with an Old Friend,
Sperry Falls, Woodbridge, Connecticut

By these falls, we pause,
laughter recalled,
folded into silence,

fifty years behind us,
our steps once long, now careful,

the rhythms we knew,
bit by bit, released,
like silt in the current,

no need to break the sound
between branches,
the pause

in the meadowlark's song.

Egyptian Revival,
West 70th Street

Two winged bulls
kneel in silence.
Not guardians—
I know now—
but thresholds.

Their flanks,
ribbed with lintel-light,`
face east—
as if remembering
the way souls rise.

Above them,
grilles catch wind
the way nets catch fish
in deeper waters.
And sometimes—
I swear—
they bring something back:
a name half-spoken,
a scent of resin,
a silence that listens.

Inside,
the elevator hums
like a funerary hymn.
I rode it once
at dusk.
A woman watered succulents
on a gilded sill.
I asked for the time.
She smiled—

as if the question itself
were already gone.

No one sees the triangle
nestled between lions.
But I do.
Its eye—unblinking—
meets mine.
A god in exile,
and not entirely alone.

Feathers and manes,
palette and plumb line—
everything repeats.
Even me.

A pigeon settles
between the wings—
not random, not tame.
It waits,
as if summoned.

And I—
passing men in earbuds,
strollers, dogs, and suits—
walk as if the pavement
hides a river.

The wind brushes
the worn edge of stone.
Something stirs—
not memory exactly,
but its echo.

This life—
seventy, eighty, ninety years—
is not the whole song.
It's the line cast
into deeper water,
the silence before
the name is spoken.

Time and Earth

Gnarled roots poking through the ground—
the knuckles of an old man

not far, a sapling's shoot
slips through the loam

I kneel beside them
press my hands into the earth

the sun warms my wrists
and the bark the same

one reaches down
where stones hold rain

the other leans into light
without knowing

On Visiting the Statue of Liberty, March 29, 2025

Seven blades rise from your crown
like reeds in the wind

severed irons at your feet—
rust sinking into stone

behind you shadows
wide enough to keep us in the dark

books unseen, unread
held in the crook of your arm

your mouth unparted—
silence hammered into edict

yet pigeons wheel above,
then vanish into sky

faint scripts of salt
gather at your hem

a thousand tongues
whisper through your seams

may you never yield—
may you never bend.

The Camino de Santiago:
Journals of Spiritual Convergence

Pilgrims

faith is not an answer—
it's a road with no signs,
no fences,
only fellow wanderers
and the sound—
of sandals on stone.

May 10, 2025—Woodbridge, Connecticut

We leave for Spain in less than one week. My wife, Ninrong, and I will walk the last stretch of the Camino de Santiago.

I am a retired psychiatrist married to a Chinese pathologist. We grew up in radically different worlds. I came of age in mid-twentieth-century America, raised in an academic family where Protestant and Catholic roots mingled with hints of Buddhism and a fascination with the foreign. Ninrong, steeped in Confucian filial piety, came of age in Mao's China, a land where science and technology were the new gods. I'm the airy type, a voracious reader of history and philosophy. She's grounded, no-nonsense. As she once quipped, "I have a spirit. I just don't talk about it."

Though unaffiliated with any religion, Ninrong is drawn to the Camino in her own quiet way. She's heard others speak of it—how it draws seekers from all walks of life—and that alone carries its own kind of allure. And while she is an MD-PhD, a scientist by training, she still prays to the wooden Buddha on our porch and believes, as she's told me, that "we go somewhere after we die." Her creed? "Common sense, moderation, kindness, compassion." She lives it too, without fanfare, without doctrine. I've never met anyone more quietly compassionate.

As for me, I'm a newly confirmed Catholic. But I remain, at heart, a child of the sixties, adrift in the crosswinds of the twenty-first century, steeped in the *śūnyatā* ("emptiness") of the Buddha, the Tao of Lao Tzu, and the agape of Jesus Christ. I dream of a coming spiritual singularity: a future where the great world religions converge, not in uniformity but in harmony, transcending systems of control and power, someday resolving our tribal, doctrinal, and philosophical differences, and living in peace.

Naive? Perhaps. But walking the Camino is my small, stubborn way of moving toward that hope, one step at a time.

Both my parents are gone. I need to set my house in order, to prepare my little bark to cross the River Styx. To face Cerberus. To meet my Maker.

May 11, 2025

The Camino fascinates me. Its history extends far back into pre-Christian times. Long before pilgrims set their feet upon this path with scallop shells around their necks and rosaries in their pockets, Celtic tribes known as the Gallaeci, living from roughly 900 to 100 BCE, wandered westward on these same routes. They carried no crucifixes. They bore no saints' names. Yet their steps fell upon the very same Galician hills and river crossings, those undulant lands between Sarria and Santiago de Compostela that Ninrong and I will soon traverse. And it is in these prehistoric roots that I begin my search for spiritual convergence.

Legend has it that the Gallaeci walked the Camino under the canopy of the Milky Way in an astral pilgrimage of rebirth. The Camino de Santiago aligns roughly with the Milky Way in certain stretches, which may have added layers of symbolic meaning. Many prehistoric societies held beliefs in cyclical rebirth and afterlife journeys. The westward direction toward the setting sun was associated with death and the otherworld, a metaphor for the end of life with a transition to another realm.

Will our pilgrimage find its shadow in these forgotten Celtic footsteps?

May 12, 2025

Today I learned that the path we will take from Sarria to Santiago passes westward through so-called *castros*—hilltop, Celtic stone settlements. In pre-Christian times these served as dwellings and ritual centers. Lugus, the radiant god of craftsmanship, oaths, and the high sun, was probably venerated in such places. His name echoes that of Lucifer, the Light-Bearer, a word later cast into Christian shadow yet deeply rooted in illumination. Soon, Ninrong and I will pass through this landscape once alive with processions to what was understood by the Gallaeci as the Edge of the World, *Finis Terrae*, now called Cape Finisterre. Long before Saint James's relics were discovered at Compostela, this western terminus was a site of sacred reckoning.

Does Christian eschatology, where the soul journeys toward its heavenly home, echo this walk toward death, transformation, and the sea's eternal embrace? It certainly seems so.

In fact, the Catholic church, in its Medieval incarnation, was a master of syncretism—the practice of constructing Christian symbols using the forms of pagan mythology. For example, the shrines of the Celtic river goddess Nabia were rebaptized as Marian fonts. Springs once guarded by nymphs or nature spirits became holy wells. Sacred oak groves, sites of Druidic divination, became locations for chapels dedicated to the Virgin Mary. Even the scallop shell, long associated with fertility and the sea, was reimagined as a symbol of pilgrimage for baptism, rebirth, and resurrection.

Moreover, traces of an earlier cosmology linger in Catholic ritual. Might the Botafumeiro, the massive swinging censor in Santiago's cathedral, reenact Celtic fire rituals that purified air and soul? Does Catholic incense recall the smoke of druidic rites, the burning of sacred herbs to invoke divine presences?

May 13, 2025

The Gallaeci lived twenty, thirty, forty years at most—brief lives—but perhaps for this very reason, they encountered death and experienced awe with an intensity we can barely imagine.

I don't mean to idealize them in the style of Rousseau. On the contrary, their lives were most likely a struggle for survival, as brief and raw as Hobbes described. In the centuries following the retreat of ice, between stone and bronze, life must have felt exposed, elemental. Unburdened by history, philosophy, and science, I imagine they lived closer to a dimension of the divine that now eludes us.

By listening to the wind, tracing the paths of birds, and studying the forms of stone along the Camino, I hope to glimpse something of their world. Might the ground beneath my feet and the sky above my head transport me, if only for a moment, back into their silence?

Then it dawns on me: is it the ritual of walking itself where the deepest continuity lies? Pilgrimage, this sacred motion, predates every religion. In moving through the land, one is changed. In pagan times, offerings were made to spirits of earth and sky to seek favor, to read one's fate. Today prayers are offered for healing, intercession, and forgiveness.

Perhaps the singularity of world religions lies not in doctrinal convergence but in the shared human longing to walk toward mystery.

May 14, 2025

Circular versus linear—which spirituality is older and why?

Spirals—these were the iconic symbols around which Galician Celtic spirituality revolved.

The tribes that inhabited the area around the Camino carved single, double, and triple spirals into stone—circular, continuous patterns, resembling what is known as triskele or three-legged spirals associated with fertility, light, and renewal. These can still be seen in prehistoric tombs, petroglyphs, and stone sanctuaries in Galicia.

What did these spirals signify? Did they symbolize cosmic cycles of life-death-rebirth, seasonal or lunar movements, the sun's path across the sky? Were they linked to Mother Earth deities or to Celtic triadic beliefs of land, sea, and sky later absorbed into Christian Trinitarian imagery? Might each turn of the spiral represent the journey of life, symbolizing different stages of existence and a continual return to a central point?

Spirals contrast with the linear movement of the Western monotheisms. Progress, hope, redemption—were such notions foreign to our prehistoric ancestors?

May 15, 2025

On the eve of my departure, I have doubts.

I woke up at 2:00 a.m. this morning with the image of a mouse scurrying into a hole in the wall. Am I like that mouse? Have I retreated into my comfort zone of Catholicism these past few years? Am I wired, as I approach life's end, to regress to the religion of my childhood? To seek solace in an illusion of metaphysical certainty, like a mouse hiding in its tiny hole, in contrast to my braver brothers and sisters who embrace a more studied agnosticism or follow what I call Western neo-Buddhism, that transformation of Eastern spirituality shorn of gods and goddesses and replaced with a more rational mindfulness?

What does it mean to have faith? Kierkegaard's proverbial leap? Or something else? Might it require a profound receptivity, a silencing of the endless inner stream of words and thoughts, allowing something or somebody to enter my life? Is this why I walk this pilgrimage? To feel the presence of God in the hills and rivers and mountains of Galicia?

May 16, 2025

Did the Gallaeci enjoy an intimacy with nature that we have lost? Have we spiritual sophisticates with our notions of transcendence— whether Buddhist or Christian—lost this intimate contact with the divinity of the natural world?

In writing poetry as spiritual practice, I have tried to find the divine in the details of nature that surround me. This requires a

silencing of inner monologues, a return to an earlier preverbal reality. Might these Celtic tribes inspire us to access this world that we have left behind?

May 17, 2025

Our day of departure has arrived.

My arc has been atypical. Many people of my generation—educated, progressive, privileged—left Christianity or Judaism in their early adulthoods to seek their spiritual fortunes in various Asian traditions—Tibetan Buddhism, southeast Asian mindfulness, Zen, tai chi. Alienated from their own culture, they turned toward the East.

I have traveled the opposite direction. Growing up with a mother who had abandoned Catholicism and embraced Hermann Hesse, Buddhism, and tai chi in the 1960s, I have returned to Catholicism, the most ancient of Christian traditions, after spending forty years immersed in Buddhism. Now I seek a synthesis, a reconciliation, a commonality, a merger between the pantheism of the Celtics, the emptiness of Buddhism, and the hope and love of Catholicism's more mystical tradition. Is that even possible?

I believe so. Because in the back of my mind, I suspect that all these "isms," cults, and creeds lie tangled up in words. Language— discursive thought– masks a deeper, more compelling reality. Hence poetry as my favored vehicle for accessing the divine; scripture, whether it be the Bible or Buddhist sutras, as metaphor. Never take religious texts literally. They are but faint echoes of something more mysterious and elusive, yet more real and rewarding than words.

May 19, 2025—Sarria

We arrive in Sarria, unremarkable at first glance, under a gray and forgiving sky—a functioning modern city. From here, the last stretch to Santiago begins. As for many pilgrims, this marks the turning of an interior key for me.

I have reached this point through a long arc. I carry not only Catholic prayers in my heart but fragments of earlier paths: the Taoist *wu wei* of effortless action; the Buddhist non-attachment of the empty bowl; the soft pantheist awe at the divine in all things. I don't discard these at the threshold of Christ's road. They walk beside me.

At a roadside cafe, we run into an Australian woman pilgrimaging from Melbourne. When I tell her that I am traveling from Buddhism to Catholicism, she quips, "not many of those." We both chuckle.

At the Iglesia de Santa Mariña, a modest church above the town, I sit before a fresco of Santiago as a Christian pilgrim. I attend a Spanish mass.

Iglesia de Santa Mariña de Sarria

I sit in the last wooden pew—
a nick in the grain
holds a thread of someone else's scarf.

Frescoes above me:
faces drowned in lime,
a hand raised,
another cupping space.

Light bleeds through glass—
red, then gold, then green—
stain my sleeve
with memories.

Voices rise,
a language I do not follow,
amen, Cristo, Sanctus
all I understand.

The priest lifts bread
and I, nothing in my hands,
feel something shift—
wind finding
a path it already knew.

We eat a modest supper of *caldo gallego* (white beans, leafy greens, chorizo) and crusty bread. The air tastes like anticipation and eucalyptus. That night, I dream of footsteps, not mine, and wake before dawn.

May 20, 2025—Morgade

Pilgrim's Apple

handed to me without a word—
round and warm from the sun,
a sweetness I don't deserve,
a kindness older than hunger

We start our walk in Sarria on a cool morning just after sunrise, Ninrong beside me, the mist lifting slowly over the hills.

I shoulder my pack, Ninrong adjusts her scarf, and we begin, not with fanfare but with the quiet shuffle of footsteps on cobblestones. I'm not sure what I'm seeking. But I know it starts here.

I carry doubt
and hope

The Galician morning smells of wet leaves and woodsmoke. I begin with a stone in my pocket, not for burden, but memory. The path coils like a Celtic spiral. Here, the land is old and thick with presences. A tiny stream murmurs under moss, and I remember: the gods were once everywhere.

We say little that first morning, only nodding to other pilgrims and stepping forward, our boots finding the soft rhythm of the earth.

First Stone

one step then another
a leaf loosens its hold
before I ask it to
each moss-covered milestone
reminds me
of things I've left unnamed

The stones beneath us are older than any single belief. Before the cross, there was the spiral. Before the incense of Mass, the smoke of solstice fires. At a bend near Barbadelo, I imagine Lugh, the Celtic god of light and craftsmanship, watching us from the forest edge. His feast, Lughnasadh, once marked these lands with rites of harvest and renewal. Their paths became our paths, their groves our cathedrals.

Beneath the Yew

the branches lean inward,
not to speak—
but to listen.

a beetle crosses my path.
I yield.

The tiny hamlet of Morgade welcomes us with a quiet humility. The rising sun casts long shadows through oak groves, and a wooden cross near the roadside bears fresh flowers. Who placed them and for what prayer? I imagine pilgrims long gone, whispering petitions to Epona, the Celtic goddess of travel and horses. In her name, perhaps, they sought safe passage.

Here I see how animist and Catholic rituals might thread together. A chapel stands beside a yew tree older than any saint's story. Ninrong pauses beneath its shade and waits for me. I venture inside and discover a long-abandoned, dilapidated stone structure whose walls are covered with graffiti messages such as "Love is all" and "You are the Camino." The altar is strewn with hand-written notes, dolls, and plastic figurines beneath a print of Mother Mary—a cave of pilgrims' ecstasy.

Tao of Faith

the path climbs
then falls
like a lung in prayer

her hand
brushes the stone
where once a spiral
held the stars—

we follow the sun
but the wind keeps turning

In Morgade we discover a lively restaurant filled with pilgrims eating tuna fish pies, cheese platters, and almond cakes washed down with beer and wine. They sure know how to have a good time. Faith without food—yes, we'll be sure to avoid that when imagining a future spiritual convergence.

May 21, 2025—Portomarín

We pass through a grove of chestnut trees with thick, gnarled trunks covered in ivy and moss. Further down the path, we find an orchard of apple trees with low spreading branches blossoming in pale white flowers. Galician *hórreos*, wooden granaries elevated on stone pillars to protect stored corn from rodents and dampness, dot our way. Their ventilation slats are painted with faded red and white geometric patterns, their stone sides graced with carved crosses.

This harmony of stone and wood enchants me. Might the Tao flow through these orchards and paths? As I place one foot in front of the other, I recall our tai chi teacher's admonition to sense the energy flowing from the earth through the "bubbling wells" in the soles of our feet, passing through the area beneath our navels, upward to the crowns of our heads. These orchards and granaries seem to embody this balance of the Tao. Does the Holy Spirit flow through this Tao, or is it the other way around?

At a wooden cross outside a chapel, I pause, not to pray, not yet, but to notice. The linearity of the crucifix contrasts with the curled ferns near my feet. Is it possible, I wonder, to walk both the straight road and the spiral at once? In the evening, I read Psalm 23, then sit in silence. Something stirs in the silence between words.

A Priori

before the cross
a circle etched
in the chapel floor—
older than time or grace

As we approach Portomarín, I spot the iridescent blue-green-black-white feathers of a magpie foraging in an open field. For the Celtic Galicians, magpies were creatures of duality, both good and bad omens, their plumage representing a balance of light and dark, life and death, bridging the earthly and spiritual realms, acting as messengers or omens. They served as protectors of travelers because of their keen awareness and loud calls that alerted people to danger. Does God speak to us through these birds?

Nagarjuna on the Camino

cracked magpie feathers scatter
in a line down our path—

left behind.

a cat slips
through a chain-link,

the sound of gravel
beneath bicycle tires,

cloud light opens
between branches.

The trail winds through dew-wet fields and under chestnut trees. My breath syncs with the rhythm of the walking. We pass pilgrims from France, Korea, Brazil. There is a camaraderie in shared silence.

I hear the faint rustle of linden trees on the banks of Rio Mino as we enter Portomarín. Is this the Tao, the Holy Spirit, or nature's divine breath passing through the air?

I feel the merging. The Catholic faith I have embraced is not a rejection of earlier beliefs but their fulfillment. I remember Thomas Merton's writings on Zen and the Tao. I recall Pseudo-Dionysius's path of unknowing and Meister Eckhart's surrender of the self. The Buddhist concept of *śūnyatā* ("emptiness") is not absence but potential.

We stop at the Church of San Nicolás, rebuilt stone by stone after the reservoir downstream swallowed the original town in 1963. I think of water reclaiming all things, of Taoism's flowing nature, of the Spirit that moves without resistance.

Bridge of Memory, Portomarín, Spain

Stone by stone
they raised the drowned church—
but the river remembers
where it first sang.

Under my feet,
old arches groan
with baptisms untold.

The past is not gone.
It is just sleeping
in a deeper channel.

May 22, 2025—Ventas de Narón

The terrain shifts today. Wind presses hard against us as we climb Alto do Poio. Ninrong pulls her scarf tighter. I let the cold bite my face.

Alto do Poio

The wind here does not follow roads.
It carves its own liturgy
through heather and bone,
through sheep-cries swallowed in mist.

A blackthorn bush bends low,
as if listening.

Even the rocks
seem to remember something
they will never say.

We pause beside a cow pasture, our breath visible. Here the wind is a god. In the time of the Celts, Taranis ruled the skies, and thunder was a hymn. Why not now too? The presence of ancient deities lingers in the air. Not discarded but transformed.

Threshold

we step through fog
where oak once stood—
a hush,
the scent of rain on wood.
no bell, no psalm—
just stones in rows,
a snail drawn slow
along the grain of God.

Before we reach Ventas de Narón, we deviate off the Camino to find the ruins of Castromaior, a prehistoric Celtic fortification built around the eighth century BCE. On a windswept ridge of rock and grass, we find a maze of ancient stone walls. I imagine how these Celts, a mixture of early agriculturalists and pastoralists practicing farming and animal husbandry, lived here 2,700 years ago during the late Bronze and early Iron Ages.

These ancient fortifications jut out of the earth like a series of ribs. I crawl down into the stony complex. Did the Gallicae huddle here to escape invading tribes or to hide from wild cats and mastodons? I don't know. But I assume theirs was a world haunted by fear, punctuated by brief moments of solace courtesy of the gods they worshiped among these hills and streams and clouds. How different are we, living in fear of nuclear annihilation, climate catastrophe, and digital oblivion, from them? Whether by worshiping a God up above or all around us, or living in the emptiness and nongrasping of the Tao or Dharma, aren't we merely trying to find our peace in a world that we can never truly understand or predict?

Castromaior

A broken ring of stone—
wind sifting through
what once held fire.

I kneel and touch the wall.
Lichen flakes off
like old skin.

The hill says nothing.
But a silence gathers,
dense as fog.

A lapwing startles upward,
wings cutting a curve
through morning stillness.

Stone to palm—
a slow pulse,
cool and wide.

No gods,
no names,
only the weight of knowing.

The ground breathes.

Somewhere in it,
so do I.

May 23, 2025—Palas de Rei

This morning on the Camino, Ninrong and I walk side by side. I pause to wait for her as we climb a hill. Young pilgrims bound past us, hiking poles swinging, their backpacks cinched tightly to their backs. Bicyclists whir by. Even the occasional farm tractor makes its way along our path. Humanity moves at its own pace, some with scallop shells, some without.

Is my search for spiritual singularity naive? Maybe we're meant to walk different paths, each at our own pace, guided by our own beliefs. Isn't that diversity something to honor, not erase?

I think of my friend from medical school who sees religion as little more than a sociobiological adaptation, a tool to organize societies, nothing more. Or those who believe that religion breeds division, drawing lines where there could be bridges. Others reject faith entirely, unable to reconcile a loving God with a world so full of pain. And there are those, millions across continents, who have simply "moved on," living fully within rational, scientific frameworks. Still others hold fiercely to the sacred particularity of their traditions, viewing any attempt to unify belief systems as idolatry or worse, heresy.

How could a global spirituality ever free itself from the weight of ritual, identity, culture, tribe, and clan? The barriers seem unshakable.

And yet I wonder. If we peer far enough ahead, a thousand or two thousand years from now, might some great rupture—a technological revolution, a planetary crisis—force us to remember what we share? That we are all humans seeking peace, love, and joy, even if we use different stories, symbols, and names to point toward the same horizon?

On the way to Palas de Rei, Ninrong befriends a Chinese-American couple in their early sixties, both highly educated, curious, and warm. We walk with them for hours, sharing a quiet sensibility. Together we pause to photograph roadside crosses, spring-fed streams, and the long tunnels of trees that shade the path.

We spot a small Romanesque chapel tucked beside the road. I enter, make the sign of the cross, and sit quietly to pray. The others linger at the doorway, taking photos of statues of Mary and Saint James, admiring the carvings and painted walls.

When we leave, I steer the conversation away from anything religious. I assume, perhaps unfairly, that they are secular progressives, global citizens more interested in language, history, and culture than in faith. We talk about architecture, the light on the fields, the curve of the trail.

And yet, I feel the silence. Why does talk of the spiritual come so uneasily? Is it just good manners that keeps us quiet or something deeper? In a secular age, have we lost a shared vocabulary for the sacred? Must spiritual life retreat behind closed doors, sealed off from society, confined to private rooms of the soul?

In Palas de Rei we visit a Romanesque church as a storm passes overhead. My legs ache. I watch an old woman light a candle beside a statue of the Virgin. She doesn't bow. She just stands there. Her stillness reminds me of zazen. No asking. Just being. The Tao doesn't strive, nor does she. I imagine Mary not as queen but as river.

Pilgrim not by feet alone -
but by every confession
left unspoken

Inside, the church is dim and full of candlelight. I think of how early Christians in this region once blended their faith with local customs, carving crosses beside sun symbols, baptizing wells once sacred to pagan deities. The Spirit moved through this syncretism.

I light a candle for the peace of our journey. I ask for blessings for Ninrong, and for our children, Allison and Danny. I speak my prayers aloud, trusting that someone hears. That God listens. That the universe is not indifferent.

Perhaps Jesus really did rise from the dead. Maybe, in the end, love will triumph over evil. I carry these hopes quietly. Is this faith? In the church, I spot a wooden carving of Jesus lying on the ground the day after his crucifixion.

We stay the night at a simple pension. I write a few lines before I fall asleep.

May 24, 2025—Melide

We wake to overcast skies and walk through the drab outskirts of Palas de Rei—tin roofs, concrete warehouses, factory yards, the echo of highway overpasses. The modern world intrudes. Europe isn't a museum. People live and work here. So much for my romantic vision of uninterrupted medieval beauty.

Soon the Camino draws us back into silence. We pass beneath chestnut trees. A rooster calls in the distance. The air carries the scent of manure and spring. Birds announce the morning—chaffinch, black-cap, robin, thrush. Shafts of sunlight filter through a canopy of linden above our heads. And as if on cue, the obligatory Romanesque chapel appears—cool, dark, and inviting. I step inside, light a candle and pray.

Which world is more real, the ancient or the modern? Which bears God's fingerprints more clearly? Why do we elevate one and dismiss the other? Must Christianity fixate on a single moment in a single place two thousand years ago? Can't the divine speak through newer voices, through data streams and overpasses, factory rhythms and LED screens? Might grace hum even in the drone of highway traffic? Or is God confined to the priest's chapel, the poet's tree, the breathless hush of incense? Or, if you lean a little further afield, to the silence of a Zen retreat?

Do our aesthetic preferences shape our theology? And if so, which sacred voices have we failed to hear?

The Camino suggests a solution. As we pass through old Galician farm villages, I notice scores of abandoned stone structures with crumbling red tile roofs alongside newer ones rebuilt in the ancient style, or most ingeniously, composite structures studded with ancient stones surrounded by new mortar. In other words, these Galicians have renovated by literally inserting the old into the new. Might this indicate one way that a global spiritual singularity might evolve in the future, by salvaging ancient insights and reconfiguring them with newer ones?

A cool drizzle follows us like a benediction. The Camino whispers in the rustle of leaves and the click of poles. I walk behind Ninrong for hours, watching the sway of her pack, the persistence in her stride. We speak little, every stone inscribed with grace.

Lord's Way

grace wears no crown—
it limps beside us,
speaking in calluses

The path from here undulates, old chestnuts forming a canopy overhead. We cross streams once central to animist rites. It is here that I think most about sacred convergence. Pilgrims once left offerings at springs. I offer silence. Ninrong, before a shrine of Mary, whispers something in Mandarin. I imagine Kuan Yin and Mary as twin spirits of compassion.

Melide is full of scents—octopus, woodsmoke, wax.

Ninrong and I sit in a tavern, elbows grazing strangers who feel like kin. The wine is cheap and generous. We speak of grace, how it might be found in fatigue, in cracked heels, in the ache behind the knee.

Between Shrines

at the spring,
a woman kneels
not to drink—
but to look
for something she lost
before she was born

above her,
an acorn falls

no one hears it
but the water

May 25, 2025—Arzúa

Leaving Melide, Ninrong and I walk through quiet streets, the air heavy with absence. No children. No strollers. Just cafes where old men nurse beers and pensioners linger in the shade, unhurried, as if time had loosened its grip. Where have the young ones gone? The town feels less like a village and more like a curated exhibit, a museum of vanished lives where we pilgrims roam, admiring the architecture and wondering what's missing.

I don't know what the future holds, but I do know this: our path is strewn with copper-speckled leaves fallen from eucalyptus trees overhead. I bend down, pick one up, and hold it to my nose. Eyes closed, I inhale a faint citrus tang, sharp and clean. I thank God for these small wonders of the Galician Spring.

The Wisdom of Sycamores

brown
green
gray
white
bark loosens—
brittle sheets
crumbling in my hands
scattered on the trail

above me—
naked trunks
peeling without shame
casting off
everything
rising
bone-pale
in the sky

When I look up, I notice bark peeling from trunks, curling in loose strips. Eucalyptus exfoliates, layer by layer. Can we, too, shed what no longer serves us, letting go of old skin, dropping our brittle leaves, reaching upward, nourished from below, lightened for the climb?

The eucalyptus groves smell like memory. One breath, and I'm back in San Francisco, a medical student jogging through Golden Gate Park, from Mount Parnassus down to the Pacific, beneath the tall, whispering trees. The scent of eucalyptus floats beside me like a silent companion.

In those years I spent my days memorizing anatomy, biochemistry, and pharmacology. But I also sat zazen at the Zen Center on Page Street and took quiet refuge at Green Gulch and Tassajara. I studied my breath. I chased stillness.

Had someone told me then that I would one day become a Catholic, I might have smiled and shaken my head. I didn't pray. I didn't own a Bible. I read the Diamond Sutra: "Form is emptiness, and emptiness is form." That was my scripture. Mindfulness was my discipline. Silence, my liturgy.

Now, almost a half century later, I stop at a tiny, roadside chapel in Galicia where a fresco of Christ's agony almost brings me to tears. Ninrong places her hand on my back. I have come a long way, from the serenity of my Buddhist mind to the contemplation of Christ's agony. Here, on the Camino, these two paths converge.

We eat lunch beneath an oak, its wide branches casting a cathedral of shadow over the dry earth. The breeze moves through the leaves like a low chant. We share what we have, cheese wrapped in wax paper, apples bruised but sweet. A German nun joins us, her habit dusty at the hem, her face weathered in a kind way. She speaks in careful English, pausing between words as if translating not just language but feeling.

"The Camino," she says, "is not the road. It is the person walking it."

I believe her. Not because I understand it fully, but because something inside me loosens when she says it, like a knot untying without effort. My legs feel steadier now, as if they've remembered what they were made for. The ache remains, but it no longer defines the walk. My doubts, once loud and insistent, fall quiet like sheep resting in the shade. The path ahead is still long, but I no longer fear its distance.

A fellow pilgrim confides in me that his knees are giving out. We walk slower, matching pace with pain. He is Irish, with a dry wit and a priestly cadence to his voice, as if every sentence were a prayer half-swallowed. As we move along the shaded path, we talk about the Book of Kells, how the monks, in their quiet defiance or perhaps unconscious devotion to memory, preserved the old pagan spirals and sun-wheels beneath the shimmering gold of the gospels. "Layers," this pilgrim says, "like sediment." Symbols upon symbols. Meaning buried in meaning.

We joke that we are both "recovering monotheists"—his phrase, not mine—trying to loosen the rigid scaffolding we inherited. Not to abandon faith, but to let it breathe. To believe again, not higher, but wider. Not firmer, but deeper. Something older than doctrine, something like moss remembering stone. As we walk, the Camino becomes less a line and more a spiral, drawing us inward even as we move forward.

Camino Tao

the gurgling of roadside brooks
the crunch of gravel beneath our feet
the silence of ivy climbing linden trees

The hills grow gentler. We stop and rest beneath a chestnut tree, and I think of Teilhard de Chardin, of his vision of the Omega Point, the divine drawing all toward itself. Perhaps this pilgrimage is drawing all of us toward such a point?

Ninrong and I reach Arzúa. We sip cappuccinos at a roadside cafe in the dappled shade beneath a spreading canopy of plane trees. Their thick trunks of mottled bark and heavily pollarded branches remind me of Vincent van Gogh's masterpiece *The Road Menders*, in which you can see plane trees with their twisted branches along a street in Saint-Remy. Sitting with Ninrong in that late afternoon sunlight beneath those plane trees, I am at peace. Perhaps all we need is sunlight, a bit of shade, and some good coffee.

Gratitude

the cheese is salty
the bread, warm
the shade smells of moss and sleep

you hand me a leaf,
torn and veined

That night, in the ancient Romanesque Iglesia de Santiago de Arzúa, I attend Spanish Mass. I understand almost nothing, yet I follow easily. The ritual is identical to the one I know back home. A nun strums a guitar. We sing hymns of cascading hallelujahs. I feel goosebumps. My body sways. I shut my eyes and let Jesus enter my beating heart. A calm settles in. I lift my gaze to statues of Mary and Saint John, gilded and painted in blue, red, and green. I receive the host, swallow the wafer—the mystical body of Christ—and return to my pew. The priest sprinkles holy water over us. I thank God for the grace of worshiping with these strangers.

Strangers? Well, not quite. These people beside me—left, right, front, and back—whose names I'll never know, are part of the same body: the Body of Christ, that invisible, unbroken communion of believers scattered across the world. Like the Eucharist itself, this body is not the physical form of Jesus of Nazareth but something larger, stranger, and more enduring. It reminds me of Mahayana Buddhism: the historical Buddha, the Buddha-nature within all beings, and the countless Buddhas shimmering across time and space. Catholicism and Buddhism differ deeply, yet here they seem to meet in what I call spiritual elasticity—the ability of truth to take on many forms across many realms.

Later that night, back at our pension, I look up the reading from Mass: John 14:27. "Peace I leave with you. My peace I give unto you: not as the world giveth, give I unto you. Let not your heart be troubled, neither let it be afraid." Almost too good to be true. But this is the miracle, if one dares the leap. Tonight, I do.

Buddha-nature, the Body of Christ, the Tao, the Holy Spirit—

on the Camino I search for where they converge. And I find it—in stone churches and lichen-covered trees, in birdsong and bread, and in the long, quiet company of pilgrims walking beside me.

May 26, 2025—Salceda

We leave our pension in Arzúa later than usual. The gray buildings of the outskirts yield to the walnut canopies of the Camino. Fruit sellers wait by the path. They are immigrants from Latin America. One woman wears what looks like a Bolivian bowler hat, a *bombín*. Could she be Quechua, finding a new life here in Spain?

Up ahead a cluster of young women from California strides past in Lululemon leggings and backward baseball caps, their English ringing loudly through the air. Moments later, a group of German men on sleek trail bikes zips by.

Soon we merge into the river of pilgrims heading west. Danish, French, Spanish, Irish, and German fill the air. The sky clears. The path flattens. I fall silent. A chorus of birds surrounds us. The way ahead is still and hushed.

A rhythm takes shape. Crowded stretches give way to moments of solitude. I find it beautiful, this shifting balance I cannot control. Whoever chooses to walk joins us. All are welcome. And most, it seems, make it to the end. Such quiet common purpose feels rare these days.

I keep walking. Perhaps there is hope.

We reach Salceda by afternoon. The town is small, a mere crossing of roads and breath. My body aches. My mind is clear. I watch swifts dart over the tiled roofs and think of the Holy Spirit, not as dove or fire, but as motion, as awareness.

I stand alone by a field of prairie grass swaying, rippling, bowing, dipping, whispering in the wind. I practice tai chi, each time sinking deeper into the ground while flowing with the wind. Perhaps this grass knows more than I do—rooted yet flexible, balanced yet yielding. There is wisdom in the silence of prairie grass.

In a small chapel, I sit alone. The Spirit here feels neither old nor new. It is a breeze through cracked windows, a rhythm in the breath. A Celtic thin place, as they say, where heaven and earth brush lips.

Texts, creeds, scriptures, statues, icons—is it possible to practice Christianity without becoming attached to these? Can I pray without words or images?

Perhaps the Holy Spirit, which seems to get the least airtime of the three aspects of the Trinity, most closely approximates this God I imagine as ethereal, flowing, ineffable—the lightness of a presence beyond energy and mass, a voice beyond voices, a Tao of faith.

May 27, 2025—O Pedrouzo

I rise a bit earlier than usual. We sip coffee outside. We linger. I feel the sun rise behind our backs. A rooster crows in the distance. Robins and sparrows warble and trill. I thank God for granting us this day. I thank God that the sun rises. I imagine the ancient Gallaeci living beneath this same sun.

A Peruvian woman stamps our Camino passports. Sitting on a plastic chair at a makeshift table in the forest, she sells Ninrong some hair bands. Further along, two young Korean women laugh animatedly, while two elderly women from Denmark with walking sticks pass us at a rapid clip, all of us swept along this route that humans have been traversing for millennia.

As we approach O Pedrouzo, I walk and meditate.

Camino Meditation

my breath steady
heartbeat
water in a clay bowl

solar plexus warm
low embers
glowing

neck and shoulders soft
earth after rain
forehead cool

the space
between my eyes
a windless field
an echo held in stone

my hips
a gate left open

In O Pedrouzo the modern and the ancient hold hands. Cafes beside stone walls. Cell phones charging beside scallop shells. I watch Ninrong sketch a swallow in her journal.

Over dinner and wine at our pension, we speak of our marriage as a pilgrimage. Of how Tao and Spirit have brought us here not to finish something, but to begin again. The world needs not a new religion but a new way of walking.

Shell and Ink

Her pen moves
like a swallow's wing
across this page—
a bird, a hill, a path.
She doesn't draw the end.
She never does.

May 28, 2025—Lavacolla

Leaving O Pedrouzo, we climb a steep hill. I meditate on my breath, even as it quickens. I recall that summer I spent in Thailand years ago, the long days in the jungle following my breath, the sensation of my belly rising and falling, my thoughts wandering then returning, that calm, deep, cool feeling. Here it's different. My breath is rapid, shallow, warm.

Following My Breath on the Camino

The uphill path breaks
what little rhythm I had—
each step a scattered chord.

This is not the breath
they taught me—soft and smooth,
cradled in silence.

In a Thai monastery
I sat cross-legged
listening for the still point.

Now breath comes raw,
stripped of form—
a rhythm of effort, not grace.

Poles scrape stone,
boots sink in loam—
no bell marks this path.

Beneath my ribs
a pulse deepens—
old, animal, raw.

A thorn snags my pant leg,
sap glistens on eucalyptus bark—
the air carries iron and resin.

Another hill,
another weight,
a man bent beneath wood.

We spend the morning in near silence, each in our own prayer. A
wild dog follows us for miles, then disappears at a crossroads. Light

filters through stained glass in a tiny chapel, hitting my face like forgiveness. I begin drafting a new poem in my head as we pass through the woods.

The pine forest closes around us. The air is blue with incense from a wayside shrine. We sit beneath a chestnut tree. I do not name God. I do not deny Her. I breathe. In and out. Just this. Eucalyptus. Manure.

Lavacolla's name speaks of washing, cleansing. I kneel and touch the cold water of a roadside stream. In medieval times, pilgrims washed here before reaching Santiago. The rite felt natural. Necessary. I remember monks in Burma walking barefoot in silence, their bowls empty, their hearts open. I remember Mass in Manhattan, incense curling like the breath of God. All of it held now in my wet hands.

We arrive in Lavacolla in the late afternoon and settle into a rambling, renovated estate, its stones over three centuries old. Behind high walls, a courtyard greets us, a gurgling fountain at its center, vines trailing along the masonry. A small Romanesque chapel opens off the courtyard, drawing me into its cool, dim interior.

I ease into a wooden pew, resting my legs. Above the altar, a gilded statue of Saint Mary catches the fading light. I close my eyes.

In the stillness, I listen. My heart speaks in fragments. In the dark quiet of the Galician countryside, I feel something vast and tender. Grace. Not spoken but known.

Ninrong and I wander the grounds. The sun drops low. Eucalyptus trees cast long shadows. The scent of blue thistle, water parsley, and aromatic aster drifts through the twilight. We hold hands.

The ancient stones, the hush, the air between day and night— there is no need for words.

May 29, 2025—Santiago de Compostela

We arrive as if from many centuries ago—Celtic, Buddhist, Christian. We enter the cathedral plaza just as the noon bells ring. We sit in the shadow of the church.

Plaza del Obradoiro or the Theodicy

a man weeps
with his head on his knees

his backpack leans
like a tired disciple

above him,
the pigeons don't care

We enter the ornate interior of the cathedral. A sea of tourists raises cell phones to the golden altar, their cameras flickering like candles, as if they could capture a piece of this mystery and bring it back home. A line forms to touch the tomb that houses Saint James's bones.

Every few minutes a disembodied voice intones, "silence please." A hush descends across the audience. A gradual crescendo re-emerges, followed by another exhortation to silence.

I enter a side room. Silence. A faint hint of incense. I settle my thoughts.

The heavy baroque, the angels from the Counter Reformation, the gold plundered from Latin America, the souls tortured for heresy—how might any of this provide for the future spiritual convergence I imagine?

And yet, it's just our luck. Today is the Feast of the Ascension, one of those rare occasions when the Botafumeiro, or giant censor, is swung. The name comes from the Galician *bota* ("to throw") and *fumeiro* ("smoke"), i.e. "smoke-thrower," referring to the giant censer used to burn incense during liturgical ceremonies. Suspended from the cathedral's central dome, it hangs from a pulley and is swung on a long rope by a group of men called *tiraboleiros*. In the Middle Ages, it was used to mask the smell of unwashed pilgrims who had walked for weeks across Europe. Today, it is used to celebrate the culmination of the journey with those who have completed the Camino.

Ninrong and I attend evening Mass to catch the spectacle of the Botafumeiro. After communion the *tiraboleiros* swing the giant pulley of the Botafumeiro. Its arc grows wider with each swing. Incense fills the air. We are awestruck.

Back at our hotel, I write a long poem. I erase it. I meditate on our sunset balcony. I hear three layers: the low hum of traffic, a midrange chorus of birds chattering in the trees, and a persistent ringing in my ears. A blackbird in the distance sings fluty, warbling notes, pierced by sharp whistles.

blackbird's trill
traffic's low river—
twilight braids their voices

Isn't spiritual life like this, a fugue of overlapping voices? The rush of traffic, the bird's song, the tinnitus, none greater than the other, each an echo of the divine, waiting to be heard?

I practice tai chi on our balcony. I balance myself—heels down, weight soft, breath sinking. I picture a line of energy emanating from the ground to the crown of my head—so different from the vaulting arches of Sainte-Chapelle, the West always straining skyward, never quite at home below.

June 1, 2025—Barcelona

We pause in Barcelona on our way back home. We make the obligatory visit to the Sagrada Familia cathedral. We arrive in the late afternoon as the sun sets. I am struck at the throngs of tourists admiring the stained glass.

The Sagrada Familia, still unfinished after a century of construction, attracts millions of visitors, making it one of the most visited monuments in the world. As for the fraction who are Catholic, my hunch is that it's small, given the diverse nature of the tourists.

I wonder—might the Sagrada Familia serve as a symbol of future spiritual globalism? Could the way Antoni Gaudí designed the basilica, with its stained glass, organic shapes, and universal themes, be seen as a reflection of a world where diverse cultures converge, not through doctrine, but through a shared aesthetic experience?

Sagrada Familia, West Nave

red gathers in the western glass—
a hush of embered air

above, vaults rise—
lungs held open after breath

color pools at the feet of those
who've stopped explaining

they say nothing
they stand and stare

as red pulls back
into the bones of the day

June 2, 2025—New York City

I try to make sense of our pilgrimage. How does it illuminate my search for spiritual convergence?

As a psychiatrist, I turn to Karl Jaspers, the great twentieth-century psychiatrist turned philosopher and his notion of the Axial Age, that profound transformation that occurred between 800 and 200 BCE, with a special focus around 500 BCE.

Jaspers proposed that during the first millennium BCE, civilizations across Eurasia, despite having no direct contact, underwent radical shifts centered on moral reflection, personal responsibility, and transcendence. Humans questioned mythological traditions and explored universal ethics, metaphysics, and the nature of the divine.

In India, Siddhartha Gautama (the Buddha) developed a path of personal liberation from suffering through mindfulness, ethics, and the Middle Way. The Upanishadic thinkers moved Hinduism toward internalized, philosophical spirituality with the identity of Atman and Brahman. In China Confucius emphasized ethical relationships, social harmony, and virtue, while Lao Tzu and Taoism proposed a mystical harmony with the Tao (Way), emphasizing minimalism and naturalness. In Greece pre-Socratic philosophers such as Heraclitus and Parmenides started asking questions about the cosmos, being, and change, while Socrates began a rational, dialogical search for truth and ethical living based on reason and introspection. In Israel the rise of the prophetic tradition ushered in a more universal ethical monotheism, emphasizing justice, mercy, and personal repentance, with the Hebrew Bible reflecting a shift from tribal law to a covenantal theology.

Why did Jaspers consider this period an axis or turning point in human history, and why does his theory intrigue me? Because, as Jaspers claimed, during these critical centuries, people became conscious of being, experiencing the absolute in the depth of their selfhood and in the clarity of transcendence. Critical self-reflection, universal ethics, and transcendental thinking were born, the foundations for later Judaism, Christianity, Islam, Hinduism, Buddhism, Taoism, and many other spiritual systems.

My hope and my question, after more than 2,500 years since the last Axial Age—might we, in the twenty-first century, find ourselves on the cusp of yet another Axial Age, one in which we embrace a new spirituality?

What might such a paradigm look like? Perhaps it might represent not a flattening of traditions into one but rather their mutual transparency, each becoming a window into the others.

Take the three traditions that have drawn my attention lately and picture them as three overlapping circles, a Venn diagram, if you will:

The First Circle—
The Polytheistic Animism of Prehistoric Galicia

The Celts, long before Christianity made landfall, held a sacred view of nature in which gods and spirits moved through trees, springs, winds, and stones. Divinity was dispersed, immanent rather than transcendent. The spiral, their enduring symbol carved into rock, signified cycles of return, continuity with the land, and a cosmos always becoming.

What survives today of their worldview is not dogma but gesture and site—hilltop castros, petroglyphs, ritual wells. Their legacy is relational, not doctrinal—a deep, reciprocal participation with nature and with the dead.

The Second Cycle—
Monotheism after Jaspers's Axial Age

With the ethical monotheism of Judaism, the Socratic rationalism of Greece, and the moral interiority of early Christianity, the divine became more personal and moral. A single God commands righteousness and reveals Himself through prophets and scriptures.

This monotheism bears linearity—creation, fall, redemption. It orients history with purpose and individuals with responsibility. Unlike the cyclical world of the Celts, this teleological universe awaits fulfillment.

Christianity, particularly in its mystical strains—Meister Eckhart, Saint John of the Cross, *The Cloud of Unknowing,* Thomas Merton—returns to silence, paradox, and surrender, echoing older ways.

The Third Circle—
Taoism and Buddhism

Though distinct, Taoism and Buddhism share a common ethos— the emptiness of forms, the futility of grasping, and the path of nonresistance. They reject the notion of a personal God, yet are profoundly spiritual, focused not on belief but on alignment, whether with the Tao or the Dharma. Buddhism offers compassion and liberation through mindfulness of suffering; Taoism offers balance through simplicity and spontaneity. Both recognize that truth lies beyond language and that striving itself is the problem.

Where monotheism provides commandments, Taoism offers

metaphors. Where Celtic spirituality invokes spirits, Buddhism watches them pass like clouds.

The Overlap—
What Common Ground Could Possibly
Unite These Three Worldviews?

MYSTERY—All three honor what is beyond comprehension, whether in the whispering groves of Galicia, the clouded mountain of Sinai, or the empty valley of the Tao.

PRACTICE—Each has rituals that transcend belief: pilgrimage, offering, fasting, silence, breath.

MORAL ORIENTATION—Though expressed differently, all three traditions recognize suffering and propose a kind of healing, be it through harmony with the land, obedience to divine law, or the cessation of craving.

AWE BEFORE THE ORDINARY—Whether in stone, sacrament, or breath, the sacred is found in the here and now.

Yes, all this invites rebuttals. It's oversimplified. It downplays irreconcilable differences. It omits culture and context.

Yet perhaps in these zones of overlap, a new beginning, a new axis might be found, an intersection that transcends language and theory and invites common ground.

June 3, 2025—Woodbridge, Connecticut

As I return to our suburban life in the forests of Connecticut, I carry a silent awareness of this new beginning with me. I am a perpetual beginner.

Not until the Camino did I understand walking itself as theology. That each step could be an invocation. That sky and bread and silence could all become sacraments.

This, I think, is what might be needed in times of religious alienation. A spirituality that moves not by argument but by presence, that is Catholic enough to break bread, Buddhist enough to let go, and Celtic enough to bless the stone.

We may never have a theology that unites them all, but we can have a shared gesture: to walk, to notice, to revere.

not a tower, but a clearing
not a doctrine, but a way
and at the center of the spiral,
stillness

 Robert Giebisch is a retired psychiatrist and world traveler with a lifelong interest in Buddhism and global spiritual traditions. His work has appeared in *The RavensPerch* and *Orenaug Mountain Poetry*. His debut poetry collection, *Geographies of Time*, was published by Shanti Arts in 2025. He lives in Woodbridge, Connecticut, and the Upper West Side of Manhattan, where he enjoys taking long walks through Central Park with his wife, Ninrong. He is a graduate of Harvard College and the University of California, San Francisco School of Medicine.

robertgiebischauthor.com

Shanti Arts

Nature • Art • Spirit

Please visit us online
to browse our entire book catalog,
including poetry collections and
non-fiction books on nature, healing,
art, and more.

Also take a look at our highly
regarded art and literary journal,
Still Point Arts Quarterly, a feast for
the eyes and the imagination—
available to download for free.

www.shantiarts.com